An Essay for

The Scottish New Towns
1947 *to* 1997

David Cowling

THE
RUTLAND
PRESS

Production Editor: David Pickering
Editorial Consultant: Duncan McAra

The Rutland Press
15 Rutland Square
Edinburgh

First Published in 1997 by The Rutland Press

Design and typesetting by In Production, Edinburgh

Printed and bound by Pillans and Wilson Greenaway, Edinburgh

Scans by Scottish Studios, Glasgow

A catalogue record for this book is available from the British Library

ISBN 1-873190-47-6

Cover: Charles Anderson's award-winning sculpture, *The Community*, Livingston Square, Livingston, photographed by Guthrie Photography, Glasgow

Contents

Acknowledgements

Author Acknowledgements

The author wishes to thank the following individuals for their invaluable assistance and encouragement:

Malcolm Allen, Colin Cowan, Ken Davie, Gordon Davies, Hugh Dobbins, Helen Leng, Derek Lyddon, John McCombie, Charles McKean, David Pickering, Roan Rutherford, William Scobie, Tony Scott, Sam Small, Sebastian Tombs and George Wren, together with a host of people resident in the Scottish New Towns whose ready conversation and pride in their towns has been invaluable.

Sponsorship Acknowledgements

Special thanks are also due to the following major donors:

Glenrothes Development Corporation

Cumbernauld Development Corporation

Livingston Development Corporation

Irvine Development Corporation

Ibstock Scottish Brick Ltd

Land Securities Plc

Picture Acknowledgements

Cover	John Guthrie Photography
Page 83	The Jesperson 'piano' blocks, Livingston Development Corporation
Page 93	Rivergate Shopping Mall, Irvine Development Corporation
Back cover	Nigel Hart Studio

All other pictures by David Cowling

Foreword

'At the beginning of the twentieth century two great new inventions took form before our eyes: the aeroplane and the Garden City; the first gave man wings and the second promised him a better dwelling place when he came down to earth'

Lewis Mumford

This book examines the unique results of that second invention in Scotland: the five New Towns – East Kilbride, Glenrothes, Cumbernauld, Livingston and Irvine – each set within its own city-region garden.

It is a much-needed essay for today since there are many lessons to be learnt which are relevant to contemporary issues. Forecasts of the increase in households in Scotland over the next ten years indicate a need for the equivalent of three New Towns. The quality of urban design is in the forefront of both political and professional debate. The administrative and creative challenge of providing new 'dwelling places' is therefore still with us.

In addition, now that these five New Towns are no longer new born but vibrant and maturing, it is fitting that their development should be recorded. There is the government's CD-ROM on all UK New Towns assembled by the Planning Exchange, and books on individual New Towns; but a study of Scotland's New Towns was missing.

The Rutland Press and the Development Corporations are to be commended for commissioning David Cowling to provide this missing review and guide to the Scottish New Towns. His verbal and visual commentary provides an architectural and urban design appraisal of the five towns with wit, insight and an ear for the human story.

I believe that those who visit the New Towns armed with this book will be able to place what they see in the context of the design and social issues experienced during the invention of the towns as dwelling places.

Derek Lyddon

Derek Lyddon
Chief Planner
Scottish Office (1967-85)

'It is not enough in our handiwork to avoid the mistakes and omissions of the past. Our responsibility, as we see it, is rather to conduct an essay in civilisation...'

(Lord Reith, New Towns Committee Report 1946)

Introduction
THE SCOTTISH NEW TOWNS

'New Towns? What New Towns? Oh - you mean the "schemes" outside Dundee, Edinburgh, Glasgow!'

Well - actually - no.

Scotland's five New Towns - East Kilbride, Glenrothes, Cumbernauld, Livingston and Irvine - are stretched across the Central Belt from Fife in the east, to Ayrshire in the west. Built in the years since the Second World War they are expressions of a major act of Government patronage.

New Towns and New Villages are not a new idea in Scotland. Many of the historic medieval burghs and coastal ports, of which the country is justly proud for their pleasing townscape, began as 'New Towns'. They were 'new' in the sense that they were 'planted' in places where no substantial community existed before.

Some were planted by the action of Royal, baronial, or ecclesiastical Charter, and by being given the right to hold a market or handle import and exports, they were assured of an economic base for their development. Thus, towns as diverse as Falkland and Newburgh, Perth and Pittenweem were, in their day, 'New Towns'.

The Olympia shopping mall in East Kilbride, Scotland's first New Town

Similarly the great landowners of the latter part of the eighteenth century created 'planned' villages as a part of the agricultural improvements which were taking place across Scotland at that time. Some landowners, such as the Duke of Argyll, simply wanted the neighbouring settlement out of sight of the 'new' castle, and therefore built a 'new' Inverary.

Industrial reformers David Dale and Robert Owen, wanting decent accommodation for their workers and families, created the planned 'model' industrial village of New Lanark around their cotton mills on the River Clyde in Lanarkshire. Even today New Lanark is regarded as an important piece of Scotland's heritage and has become a major tourist destination.

The five New Towns referred to above, however, were developed under the direction of public bodies called Development Corporations, which were established as an act of Government policy, and enabled by legislation, principally in the form of the New Towns Act of 1946 (subsequently amended by the New Towns [Scotland] Act 1968).

At the end of 1996 the last of these Development Corporations were wound up, and their assets and activities

The Kingdom shopping mall in Glenrothes, Kingdom of Fife

The town centre in Cumbernauld

**The Almondvale Centre, Livingston;
'Make it in Livingston!'**

**The shopping mall in Irvine;
an old New Town by the sea**

passed variously into the hands of others. Fifty years have elapsed since the first of these towns, East Kilbride, was started. They represent a large-scale public patronage of architecture, embracing not only the design of single buildings but the creation of whole new communities. This, then, is an appropriate time to consider their achievements.

In 1946 the New Towns were seen as a part of the brave new culture of that confident post-war period, when British society was unanimous in its recognition of the need to address old problems of housing failure and inner city overcrowding. These were problems which had only been made worse by the effects of the war itself. The New Towns were to be at the leading edge of a buoyant sense of enterprise and self-belief within our society. Emigrants from the crowded urban areas, freed from the unhealthy city core, were to be pioneers in new communities of opportunity in the nearby countryside. Beneficiaries of healthy fresh air, open space, trees, an easy access to the fields and hills, and participants in a new 'clean' industrial future. They were to be harbingers of a national liberation from the 'dark satanic mills'.

In turn they were to provide the cities with the 'space' to renew themselves.

The purpose of this short book is to look at the extent to which the hopes and aspirations of the post-war generation have been fulfilled, as their grandchildren and great-grandchildren contemplate their surroundings in Scotland's New Towns. It is about the story of the patronage which 'planted' the towns, the architecture which has given them form, and some of the people whose gifts have been employed in their creation.

Chapter One
GARDEN CITIES OF TOMORROW

The growth of the great Victorian cities in Britain during the nineteenth century created politically powerful entities with enormous civic pride. Nevertheless, their inherent problems of overcrowding and poor living conditions spawned an interest amongst an informed and concerned minority for the rediscovery of the countryside, and for all the benefits - clean air and growing things - which the countryside was held to represent.

The century had seen a steady stream of emigration from the countryside to the cities, driven by the Industrial Revolution and by changing agricultural practices within the countryside itself. The industrial towns and cities, famed for their civic developments, also became places of overcrowding. Despite the efforts to improve the lot of the poor in the cities, as the century neared its end there was a strong sense that there were problems which still needed to be addressed. One contemporary commentator, Dean Farrer, wrote of Britain:

Falkland: granted a Royal Charter in 1458 and built around a Royal Palace

> We are becoming a land of great cities, villages are stationary or receding; cities are enormously increasing. And if it be true that great cities tend more and more to become the graves of the physique of our race, can we wonder at it when we see the houses so foul, so squalid, so ill-drained, so vitiated by neglect and dirt?

Notwithstanding the campaigns for legislation and action which would address some of the problems of the cities within the cities - legislation regarding foul drainage, fresh water, minimum standard by-law housing etc. - a 'movement' developed to see the creation of new, planned and self-sustaining communities within the countryside. Communities which would in turn create new opportunities within the cities themselves by relieving the stress of their overcrowding.

At the turn of the century this proposal was particularly articulated by Ebenezer Howard, a clerk in the House of Commons, who was part of an intellectual concern within a section of the middle classes who desired to see change. In 1902 in his seminal book, *Garden Cities of Tomorrow* he not only set out a series of ideas for change, but also a prospectus for such a new community which would see them put into effect. This first 'Garden City' was to be at Letchworth in Hertfordshire on the Great Northern Railway, some 35 miles, and forty minutes,

Pittenweem: a picturesque fishing village in Fife, granted a Royal Charter in 1541

north of the King's Cross terminal in London. Howard was a very practical reformer.

The success of Letchworth led to the building of a second venture, Welwyn Garden City, some 10 miles nearer to the metropolis, although the First World War was to delay its start until the early 1920s. These 'New Towns' were developed by private finance, using existing legislation. They were even expected to pay a dividend. The resulting 'Garden City' environments, however, both defined a 'suburban' style, and planted 'New Towns' firmly in the British consciousness. They were also testimony to the skills of the architect, Raymond Unwin.

Scottish private house builders were keen to take up the term 'Garden Suburb' to describe the kind of housing which many of them would build on the periphery of existing towns and cities between the wars, and even before the First World War.

Lewis Mumford, 'thinker and writer about planned and unplanned society', wrote retrospectively in 1961 of Ebenezer Howard's vision, in his book *The City in History*:

> So in time a sufficient proportion of the metropolitan population would be drawn off to lower land values and make possible the reconstruction of the historic centre on more open lines, and with greater respect for health, social convenience and amenity. The success of the new Garden City would give back to the overcrowded centre the fresh air, sunlight, and beauty that its own inordinate growth had robbed it of.

Sir Patrick Geddes, pioneer Scottish town planner, writing in 1915 in his book *Cities in Evolution*, echoed Howard's vision, but from a slightly different perspective: '... for must not swifter and cheaper communications loosen out the crowded city, and so serve all its interests most efficiently in the long term'.

Inverary: a planned settlement of the mid-18th century on the shores of Loch Fyne

New Lanark: a 'model' industrial village on the banks of the Clyde

Rosyth: built on the river Forth to house Royal Dockyard workers

It is indeed difficult to imagine Howard's passion to build his 'Garden Cities of Tomorrow' without the existence of fast, regular train services or, indeed, the building of the post-war New Towns without both road and rail transport.

Meanwhile in Scotland, parallel with these southern events, Rosyth in Fife was constructed to house the workers at the new Naval Dockyard which was developed on the north bank of the Forth as a part of the arms build-up in the years leading to the First World War. Building began in 1915 under the direction of the Scottish National Housing Company, a Government Agency, which continued with its task when its activities were superseded by the Scottish Special Housing Association. Much of the earlier housing in Rosyth was contemporary with Letchworth and has the unmistakable appearance of the style developed there by its architect Raymond Unwin.

Rosyth: a touch of English bricks and Garden Suburbs

During the late 1930s, however, the Government began to react to contiguous suburban growth of the major towns and cities which better transport allowed - 'Garden Suburbs' or not. It set up in 1937 a Royal Commission, chaired by Sir Montague Barlow, to inquire into the distribution of the industrial population. By the time this Commission reported in 1940 Britain was at war again, and its principal areas of population and industrial production were being bombed by the *Luftwaffe*. The 'Barlow Report', as it became known, discussed and reported upon 'the merits of new towns in relation to the alleged advantages of continual suburban development', which had become a feature of the expansion of the cities during the 1920s and 1930s.

During the Second World War itself there were people in government who were thinking about the rebuilding of a post-war Britain. Thus in October 1945, after the election of the new Labour Government led by the Prime Minister, Clement Attlee, a 'New Towns Committee' was set up under the chairmanship of the Scot, Lord Reith, first Chairman of the BBC. Its remit was: 'To consider the general questions of the establishment, development, organisation and administration that will arise in the promotion of New Towns in furtherance of a policy of planned decentralisation from congested urban areas'. So decentralisation was to be at the heart of the new policy, echoing Howard's thesis of half a century earlier. The New Towns were to be 'developed as self-contained and balanced communities for work and living'. They were *not* to be suburbs.

In recognition that this was a whole United Kingdom issue the Committee had two members appointed specifically to represent Scotland: Sinclair Shaw and Captain J.P. Younger. The Committee presented its report to Lewis Silkin, Minister of Town & Country Planning, and Joseph Westwood, Secretary of State for Scotland, in the short timescale of three months - such was the urgency. The vision of the Report was immense:

> It is not enough in our handiwork to avoid the mistakes and omissions of the past. Our responsibility, as we see it, is rather to conduct an essay in civilisation, by seizing an opportunity to design, evolve and carry into execution for the benefit of coming generations the means for a happy and gracious way of life.

The means of achieving this utopian task was to be through the creation of Development Corporations, with their members appointed directly by the Minister or Secretary of State, rather than by 'election'. The new Corporations were to have an important 'power'. They were to be able to purchase land at 'existing use' value.

This land could then in turn be allocated to particular uses, all in accordance with plans made, submitted to, and approved by the Secretary of State. The Corporations were to be able to build housing (and later also factories), but to this extent their powers were limited.

All else depended upon the 'statutory authorities' working in partnership with them - thus roads, drains, schools, health facilities etc., were all to be procured in this way. Eventually the Corporations were also to develop partnerships with the private sector for the procurement of town centres, leisure facilities and much else. In due course also the Corporations were granted 'Special Development Orders' which allowed them to become their own Planning Authorities.

The sense of urgency, and the desire for innovation was reflected in the Committee's conclusions as to the kind of people who should be appointed to the Boards of the Development Corporations:

> The field of choice should not be restricted to 'safe' men with established public reputations: we recommend that the field should be widened to include younger people with drive and imagination and a desire to render public service.

By the end of 1946 all had been enshrined in the New Towns Act, which 'as applied to Scotland' was modified to take account of the different legal, legislative, administrative and local government systems in place here. The problems in Scotland were as acute as in the south-east of England. The New Towns Act was to be a tool soon put to work here. But then the concept of the State sponsoring a New Town development was not a new one to the Scots, as had been demonstrated at Rosyth.

Nor was the notion of 'balanced' communities located in the countryside one which lacked supporters here. There had been a strong sense in Scotland that this was a way forward, with advocates such as Councillor Mrs Jean Mann who had been the Housing Convener of Glasgow City Council in the mid-1930s. She was a supporter of the Town and Country Planning Association which had been born out of Howard's original work.

The Clyde Valley Regional Plan, prepared at the behest of the Secretary of State, by Sir Patrick Abercrombie and published in 1946, proposed the construction of four such New Towns on the periphery of Glasgow - at East Kilbride, Cumbernauld, Bishopton and Houston - to house up to 250,000 people to be relocated from Glasgow. The city had a major 'overcrowding' problem, with more than half its population living below the space standards set out in legislation enacted in the 1930s. Taking a quarter of a million people away was seen as an opportunity for the city to resolve its own problems and to recreate itself.

A parallel study set up by the Secretary of State in central and eastern Scotland, under the direction of Sir Frank Mears, saw the creation of New Towns in the east of the country as being more appropriately related to the development of the mining industry in the Lothians and Fife. There were to be three - in Woodside (now Glenrothes), Cardenden and Kennoway, all in Fife, and in Dalkeith to the south of Edinburgh. But at a projected population of some 10,000-15,000 each, they were conceived as being far smaller than the New Towns of the west which were to share a population of 250,000! The City of Edinburgh, however, did not see New Towns on its periphery as being necessary, and the Dalkeith proposal was dropped.

Edinburgh: Scotland's famous classical 18th-century New Town, now engulfed by the modern city

East Kilbride: the village around which a New Town was built

Leslie, Fife: the town which declined to join the New Town of Glenrothes

Cumbernauld: The Wynd in the village which gave its name to a New Town

Livingston Village: now surrounded by its own New Town

Meanwhile in 1947 in the west, East Kilbride was designated as a New Town under the new Act. It was not to the immediate comfort of the City of Glasgow, which had anticipated being able to solve the city's housing crisis within its own boundaries extended into the green belt.

In the east, the Secretary of State, Joseph Westwood, had announced the designation of a New Town in Fife, between Cowdenbeath and Lochgelly; but it was never to be realised. Instead, Glenrothes was designated in 1948. It was to be designed as a 'balanced community' also serving the anticipated new mining population in Fife. East Kilbride and Glenrothes thus share their 'designations' in time with many of the London 'ring' of New Towns, such as Stevenage, Harlow and Hemel Hempstead. This first round of New Towns designated under the New Towns Act shared many of the 'Garden City' qualities of Letchworth and Welwyn.

In Scotland, however, by 1953 the site at Cumbernauld was revived as a solution to the continuing problems of Glasgow 'overspill'. It was designated as a New Town in 1956, and was to be sited some 13 miles to the east of Glasgow on a hill top between the villages of Condorrat and Cumbernauld. Its planning and design marked a significant departure from what had gone before.

Livingston in West Lothian was designated in 1962 in response to the continuing crisis of Glasgow's overspill population, but it was also given an important strategic role in the revitalisation of the economy of West Lothian. It was also closer to Edinburgh than to Glasgow.

Irvine, however, the designation of which in 1966 was in large part a response to the pressure for Government help in

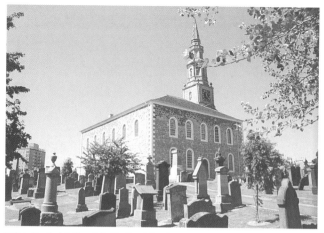

Irvine: the Parish Church in the Royal Burgh

the revitalisation of north Ayrshire, marked a major change in the use of the New Towns Act in Scotland, in that the designated area covered the existing substantial and historic burghs of Irvine and Kilwinning. In effect the New Towns Act was used here to achieve a 'town development' scheme.

This was almost the culmination of the purpose of the New Towns Act in Scotland. Times were changing, and there was an increasing awareness of the need to plough scarce and limited resources into the redevelopment of the major cities and towns. Nevertheless, in 1972 a New Town was designated at Stonehouse in the Clyde Valley. It was to be developed by the staff of the existing East Kilbride Development Corporation, which was renamed the East Kilbride and Stonehouse Development Corporation for the purpose. But the time had run out, and despite a very public commitment from the then Conservative Prime Minister, Edward Heath, the designation was cancelled by the Labour Government in 1976.

Although the Development Corporation in East Kilbride still had almost twenty years to run, many of the staff who had worked on Stonehouse were to find themselves instead working for the new Scottish Development Agency on the redevelopment of the East End of Glasgow, known as GEAR: Glasgow East Area Renewal.

It would be twenty years before the last of the five Scottish Development Corporations would be deemed to have completed its task and therefore be wound up. But there would be no new 'designations' of New Towns in the countryside, or even revivals of historic burghs. The principle of the Development Corporation as an agency for direct Government action was to be revived in the 1980s by the new Conservative

East Kilbride: the town centre before the Olympia and Plaza malls were built; Princes Square is on the right

Dalgety Bay: a private enterprise New Town near the Forth Road Bridge

Dalgety Bay: private-sector building at St David's Harbour

Administration of Margaret Thatcher. But they were Urban Development Corporations, to be used in the recovery of blighted areas of urban England and Wales. There was to be none in Scotland.

There have, of course, been other developments of New Towns of a sort in Scotland during the post-war period. For instance, Erskine on the Clyde was developed by the Scottish Special Housing Association. Dalgety Bay on the Fife coast of the Forth, was started in the 1960s and was developed by the private sector, and with the encouragement of the County Council, in response to the opportunities created by the opening of the Forth Road Bridge. It is still developing.

The five New Towns, however, of East Kilbride, Glenrothes, Cumbernauld, Livingston and Irvine, remain as the built examples in Scotland of a conscious attempt to direct Government patronage to the building of new communities. Writing in 1947, Lewis Silkin, Socialist and Minister of Town & Country Planning in England, described the task of building the New Towns in the following terms:

> The building of a new town is not merely a great task of physical construction; it is also a great adventure in social construction, for the new towns must be lively communities with their own civic consciousness and civic pride. Great responsibilities, therefore, rest with those who will administer the Act.

This was high vision indeed.

It has taken fifty years to bring that vision to anything like fruition in Scotland, and even now the New Towns are in a constant state of change and development. Fifty years has meant that the change of successive Governments and economic circumstances have led to continual changes in the objectives established for the towns. Thus, from overspill to linchpin of both local and national economic and industrial

Cumbernauld: the visionary 'mega' centre rises from the hilltop in 1964

growth, from the relief of cities to fine communities in their own right, the New Towns have changed for ever the face of central Scotland.

Lewis Mumford wrote in 1961 of the New Towns in England and Sweden:

> The very existence of the New Towns ... though they have not yet altered the dominant metropolitan pattern, still bear witness to the possibility of a different mode of urban growth. That small sign may be the harbinger of a larger transformation.

In Scotland, fifty years on from the designation of East Kilbride, we have the opportunity to form a judgement as to whether or not the Scottish New Towns have been 'the harbingers of a larger transformation'. They brought with them the powers of Parliament to develop their towns on land acquired at 'existing use' prices - a developer's dream. They invested architects and other designers with vast responsibilities and considerable patronage - an architect's dream! They involved the investment of rather a lot of money, although each was expected eventually to break even, and even to show a profit. Their creation represents a unique story of a continuing public policy sustained over more than half a century.

Only time will tell if they are also sustainable urban forms.

Chapter Two
EAST KILBRIDE – *Scotland's First New Town*

EAST KILBRIDE

N

to Glasgow
Kingsgate Shopping
Stewartfield Loch
Stewartfield Way
to M74 →
A725
to Paisley
A726
Nerston Industrial Estate
Calderwood
College Milton
Village
East Mains
Peel Park
West Mains
St Leonards
Westwood
The Murray
Birniehill
Newlandsmuir
Greenhills
Kelvin Ind. Estate
Whitehills
to Strathaven
◎ Railway Station
•‡• Town Centre
Kelvin South

- *Location:* South Lanarkshire

- *Designated:* 1947

- *Area:* 10,250 acres

- *Population:* 70,000

More jobs for East Kilbride: Abercrombie House, built by the Development Corporation for the Overseas Development Agency

Housing towers ride above the Nerston Industrial Estate

INTRODUCTION

East Kilbride is a vibrant and energetic town. Now the sixth largest town in Scotland it exudes confidence. Its apparent success is palpable.

A population of over 70,000 lives in a community of considerable cultural depth and vitality, as is shown by the range of facilities and activities which it supports.

Generation has followed generation since the first residents moved into houses alongside the old village of East Kilbride in 1950.

One resident described the process of community formation thus: 'I came here at the beginning with my parents, and then our granny came out from Glasgow to join us; now I am a granny, too, with my family around me.' Conversation with residents of East Kilbride demonstrates a considerable loyalty and pride of place, especially amongst those who consider themselves to be amongst its 'pioneers'.

There is a buzz about the place!

It always seems that whatever time of day or night that East Kilbride is visited, or passed through, the roads will be busy with traffic. The town centre appears for ever to be thronged with people taking advantage of the many facilities it has to offer, quite apart from its ample shopping opportunities. Not that the town lacks its social problems, at least partly evidenced by the graffiti sprayed and vandalised pedestrian underpasses on the approaches to the centre. But East Kilbride is underpinned by more than 33,000 jobs within its boundaries - more than one for every house in the place. East Kilbride is crisp and generally well maintained. It is testimony not only to its residents, but also to the Development Corporation which brought it into being, and to the countless numbers of people who have been engaged in its creation.

THE LOCATION

East Kilbride is situated in west central Scotland some 8 miles to the west of the M74 which forms the main road artery between the west of Scotland and the south. It is accessed by the A725 from the M74.

The northern boundaries of East Kilbride lie only a meagre 2-3 miles to the south of the southern reaches of the Glasgow conurbation. Paisley lies 10 miles to its north-east, the planned eighteenth-century village of Eaglesham just beyond its boundary to the south-west, and the small town of Strathaven 8 miles to the south.

It is located in an undulating upland topography, the elevation of which gives it an exposed position relative to the prevailing weather systems of the west of Scotland. It is visible from some distance from both the west, east and south, in part because of the location of its squat tower blocks on its eastern flank. These are seen when travelling south on the M73 and approaching that road's junction with the M74 - East Kilbride is seen rising prominently to the west. Approaching from the south-west over Fenwick Muir, East Kilbride is seen in the middle distance to be spread out across the landscape.

The 'boundary' sculpture announces East Kilbride to those coming from Paisley

Pedestrian underpass beneath the Kingsway - a refuge for those who draw on walls

Stainless steel at the Priestknowe Roundabout

Churchill Avenue, with flowers, approaches the Town Centre

English brick comes to town on the Crooked Lum Beefeater Restaurant at the Murray Roundabout

The Stewartfield Neighbourhood Centre is made for people who travel by car

THE STORY

The village of East Kilbride was one of the four sites in and around Glasgow considered suitable for the development of a New Town in the Clyde Valley Regional Plan of 1946, their purpose being to relieve the pressure of overcrowding in the city. With the passing into law in 1946 of the New Towns Act, East Kilbride was seen by the Scottish Office as being the location of the first New Town to be designated in Scotland.

The city fathers of Glasgow were well aware of the problems facing their city at the end of the Second World War, but were confident that those problems could be resolved by the city itself within its own boundaries. At the same time that the new Labour Government had been driving through its New Towns legislation, the Glasgow City Engineer, Robert Bruce, had been preparing a visionary Plan for the reconstruction of a 'self-contained' Glasgow. Basically this comprised the demolition and clearance of some of the worst of the inner-city slums, and their replacement at a lower density with flats, largely in high-rise developments. The subsequent 'overspill' population was to be housed in cottage-style properties within extended boundaries upon the periphery of the city.

The year 1946, therefore, saw the coincidence of the passing into law of the New Towns Act, the publication of the interim Clyde Valley Regional Plan, and the Bruce Plan for the City of Glasgow. They were far from being mutually compatible. The Regional Plan put a green belt around Glasgow, thus inhibiting Bruce's design; whilst the New Towns Act made possible the development of East Kilbride as a separate and balanced New Town, described in the Regional Plan as a 'residential area and industrial zone'. This designation was opposed by the city fathers of Glasgow.

The 'brick developer' Stroud Tavern at Whitehills

Hunter High School: part of the high-quality provision of schools made by Lanarkshire County Council and Strathclyde Regional Council

In the event compromise prevailed. East Kilbride was designated on 6 May 1947. Glasgow saw some extension of its boundaries, and did develop its own overspill schemes on its periphery. One of the consequences, however, was that in the early years of the New Town the East Kilbride Development Corporation gave houses only to people who had jobs in the town, and the greater proportion of its early population came from other parts of Lanarkshire.

The first Chairman of the Development Corporation was Sir Patrick Dollan, until a year before a member of the Glasgow City Council , and a former Lord Provost of the City. Like some of the English New Towns of the same era, the Corporation turned to the armed forces for its first General Manager: Major-General Dixon, a retired Royal Engineer. The first Chief Architect & Planning Officer was Donald Reay, who was followed by F.C.Scott, who had been Chief Architect in the Glasgow City Housing Department. The Secretary of State for Scotland, Joseph Westwood, considered the whole affair to be so important that he attended the first meeting of the Development Corporation Board in August 1947.

THE PLAN

The first master plan for the town was prepared by town planners in the Scottish Office and published in 1950. The plan was essentially similar to the concurrent New Towns of the south-east of England. It provided for a town centre accessed by the principal roads, with the housing gathered into

Not a revolution: flats at Maxwellton Avenue

The Whirlies whirl on the Whirlies Roundabout

The Calder and Clyde multi-storey towers from New Common Road

The lower pedestrian entrance to the Olympia Centre through the car park

neighbourhoods, each with its own secondary centre and linked to the other parts of the town by distributor roads. Industry was similarly grouped into zones for that purpose, and linked to the distributor road system. The principal road junctions in the early part of the town were by roundabouts with the pedestrian routes passing beneath.

The target population was to be 50,000 people; raised in 1960 to 70,000; and in 1969 to 82,500. In practice, lower densities of development have meant that it is at present just over 70,000.

The plan of the town has developed over the years, with, for example, the designation of additional neighbourhoods such as Greenhills and Stewartfield, new industrial visions at Peel Park, and the outer ring road. Most recently the famous Whirlies roundabout has been bypassed with a new grade-separated link between the ring road and expressway to the M74.

Over the life of the Development Corporation there have been several attempts to extend the Glasgow rail link into the town centre, and to provide a proper transport interchange with the bus system. On each occasion this has failed, and East Kilbride is essentially a bus and car town. The potential for the kind of integration, taken for granted in post-war Scandinavian New Towns, has now apparently been lost for ever. The heart of East Kilbride, however, is its town centre, and that is where roads and public transport lead.

THE TOWN CENTRE

If the key to East Kilbride's success is its successful attraction of industry and commerce, then its heart is its town centre, now one of the main regional shopping centres on the south side of Glasgow. The site of the principal retail areas is bounded by roads, which both give access to it and cast a limit around it. The town centre was originally laid out on much the same pattern as the early English New Towns, with open pedestrian streets and squares, bounded by shops, and with a limited penetration by cars and public transport. In recent years it has been successively redeveloped with a series of new indoor shopping malls: the Plaza and the Olympia and Princes Malls. The diversity, however, of the older town centre has been maintained and other uses, such as hotels, remain within the core.

Externally, the town centre presents itself as a sometimes untidy collection of buildings and the backs of buildings. Most architectural styles of the last five decades are represented here. The Plaza Tower, however, the remaining town centre office tower, gives it vertical identity and location within the town.

The 'tunnel' entrance to the Plaza Centre from the surface car park

Norfolk House, which once housed the Development Corporation, and Centre One, the home for some 1600 Inland Revenue workers, have been demolished - the latter having been removed to a new building adjacent to the Peel Park Campus.

The principal point of pedestrian access to the town centre is from the bus station through the Princes Mall. Until recently this still led into the open-air Princes Square, which used to contain the famous 'mushroom' café, run by Reo Stakis. The Square, however, is now newly roofed over to provide the heart of the indoor shopping experience.

THE TOWN CENTRE MALLS

The Plaza Mall, opened in 1973, was a major departure from the open-air shopping centre of the 1950s and 1960s. It was a mould-breaking exercise and attracted Marks & Spencer to the town. In comparison, however, with the later Olympia Mall it is relatively dark and claustrophobic. The pedestrian access to it for motorists parking to the west of the centre is via a downhill path leading to a bunker-like approach and flanked with 'prison' gates! The Plaza meets the Olympia at a pleasant banner-hung square with natural top illumination.

The Olympia, by contrast to the Plaza, is high-tech and state of the art. It was formally opened in 1990 and has been widely recognised as being at the forefront of contemporary shopping centre design. Top natural light and white modelled surfaces, with a skilful use of internal landscape, give it an apparent relationship to the 'outside' world which, although it

The Olympia mall: sunlight, shelter, shops and shoppers

'A reflection of growth' in the Olympia Centre

The Olympia Mall: exit to the car parks

The street entrance to the Olympia Ice Rink

The municipal fire station in Cornwall Street

The well-landscaped public square with the Civic Centre in the background

A 'faraway' country cottage on the edge of the town centre

cannot actually be seen, is evidenced by the pleasing penetration of sunlight. There is a clever use of reflective surfaces so that the eye is not always sure what plane is being looked at. The ambience is bright and expansive. Space is skilfully ordered, and differing levels, spaces and vistas are worked together to offer both seclusion and surprise, as a part of the spacious and shopper-friendly pedestrian malls. The main mall manages to encompass a gentle slope within its design to cope with the changes of ground level. There is a short mall of 'old world' shopfronts on a spur to the bus station. The Olympia also contains cinemas, pubs, restaurants and the magnificent ice rink, which alone represents a key magnet for both participants and spectators - and also having the advantage of the adjacent food court.

THE WIDER TOWN CENTRE

Cornwall Street essentially separates the mixed 'retail and social' town centre from the Civic Centre, opened in 1968. This was built by the former Burgh Council to serve both as a civic facility for the town and as an administrative headquarters. This is a concrete panel structure of its time - grey in sunshine, and virtually black in cloud or rain.

The bus station is a simple circular layout with the stands protected by elegant black steel and curved perspex canopies - the principal one in a curved layout. Midway between it and the Civic Centre is a sunken and circular paved court, bounded by lush landscaping which largely shields the pedestrian from the passing traffic at the higher level. Lying on one of the principal pedestrian routes into the town centre it provides a sheltered and full sunlit Town Square.

Andrew Street and Cornwall Street offer a more 'normal' town centre streetscape, the former being home to the municipal architecture fire station. Just beyond the central area itself to the north, rising out of extensive grassland and trees, is the Dollan Aqua Centre with its Olympic-sized swimming pool and grand arched design.

The Bruce Hotel in Cornwall Street

TOWN CENTRE SUMMARY

The development and redevelopment of the town centre in East Kilbride has made it into one of the most successful regional centres in Scotland. It is a true beating heart to the East Kilbride community. It is confident and apparently ever evolving. There is little doubt, however, that its present success is in large part due to its ability to change with the culture around it. At the heart of this kind of change has been the Development Corporation which not only gave it birth, but nurtured, loved it and ensured that it grew from being a child into a mature and diverse adult.

The Dollan Aqua Centre in parkland adjacent to the town centre

Cars and classical at the out-of-town Kingsgate Retail Park

The task is never complete - the builders move into Princes Square

THE KINGSGATE RETAIL PARK

In 1994 with the 'full up' signs beginning to appear in the town centre, the Development Corporation turned its attention to the development of the Kingsgate Retail Park on the northern periphery of the town. Its location made it alluringly close to the southern reaches of the Glasgow conurbation. In this sense it is effectively an out-of-town shopping centre designed to cater principally for the motorised customer.

Laid out around a large and well-landscaped car park, its retail mix is anchored in a Sainsbury's supermarket and a Texas Homecare store, with a range of other outlets all supported by

19

Tubular pedestrian porches in the Kingsgate Retail Park

a Pizza Hut and Burger King. It has been done in many other towns around Scotland. This one at least has been done well. The architecture of the whole is utilitarian pop art, the kind that says, 'I won't actually be here very long, before another bigger, brighter and better one comes along!' It ranges from 'Sainsbury classical' to glazed white tubular shelters for the motoring family.

Across the road from the Kingsgate is the Kingsgate Still, a public house and restaurant in the modern 'low, brown and pitched' style, complete with generous play facilities for children and landmark 'copper still' sculpture to advertise its presence. The way to the Kingsgate is marked by large signs in the American mode, so that none should pass this way and miss what is a remarkably complete 'family day out' shopping experience.

THE TOWNSCAPE

General

Visitors to the town will make their acquaintance with East Kilbride from the road system, and from there make their first observation of the townscape of this 'first' of Scotland's New Towns. Only a longer association will turn the visitor into a pedestrian and allow him or her a fuller observation of the ambient environment of this busy town. The undulating topography affords views both 'in' and 'out', with plenty of opportunity to view one part of the town from another, and

The 'way' for pedestrians and bicycles leads to the Whitemoss Roundabout

also to look out at the surrounding countryside.

The impression of the older parts of the town is of low-rise housing, walk-up flats and carefully sited squat tower blocks. Colours are varieties of shades of grey for walls and topped by grey, brown, and even red roofs. There is some interrupting

The busy bus station with the Civic Centre in the background

Shaded pedestrian route seen from St Leonard's Road

colour on walls, and a notable tendency for terraces to 'climb' up the contours of the low hills, making virtual giant staircases of their stepped roofs. The palette from which the townscape is created, however, changes significantly in those places where the later areas of private housing are located. The colour ranges change from grey to brown and red.

The town centre punctuates the skyline with the Plaza Office Tower and the Civic Centre, and a little to its east a group of 16/20-storey blocks of flats overlooking the town's only major grade-separated road interchange.

Landscaping

Landscaping generally has both preserved and strengthened what was good, with plenty of trees being planted, and a varied use of flowering shrubs. Mown grass is a distinct feature, and

Neat, green playing fields, edged with housing at Calderwood

House and hedges at Kelvin Road, Birniehill

impenetrable hedges a memorable way of keeping functions and uses apart. The first impression is the use of major areas of now mature tree planting, creating a constant punctuation and framing of the built development. The trees are reinforced by ample and well-maintained open space, comprising parkland, playing fields and school grounds, etc. The town is also interspersed with fingers of green following both major pedestrian routes and watercourses.

East Kilbride Village and Maxwellton

The development of the town centre and adjacent road system has left pockets of the older residential areas which predated the designation, so that, for example, 'country cottages' whose ambience is frankly 'distant rural', exist within a stone's throw of the bustling town centre. It lends an unreal dimension to the nature of the place which is delightful to the pedestrian explorer.

The East Kilbride Village 'conservation' area

The existing villages of East Kilbride and Maxwellton are now Conservation Areas. Neat and tidy 'original' places with appropriate 'old world' street furniture and lamp standards, with well-mannered infill development and polite paving in the modern manner.

The old village has a very 'conservation' feel about it; restored with cobbles, causies and cast-iron bollards! Trim, neat, illuminated, and ever so slightly unreal, and all focused on the old parish church with its St Giles-style lantern crown atop a squat tower leaning on a presbyterian box. The early and contemporary infill housing in Main Street is entirely appropriate, balustrated flats and all.

Weeding the lawn, Lindsay Place, East Mains

Early housing at Threshold, East Mains

Modern catering at the Lodge Inn, Queensway

The Neighbourhoods

Each of the neighbourhoods has at its heart a neighbourhood centre as a part of the hierarchy of shopping and service opportunities. The earliest are models of pedestrian squares with shops located under residential flats, the whole forming sheltered squares with landscape, sculpture, pubs and bus stops. The older centres are also the location for some splendid churches and social buildings from the halcyon years of the 1960s and 1970s when it was possible to afford such things.

The 'flamboyant seventies' Church of Scotland Parish Church at St Leonards

By the time, however, that the Stewartfield Centre was built the neighbourhood centre was a supermarket, a large car park, and a petrol filling station, with adjacent community centre on a separate site. Changing times and changing expectations!

One of the many strengths of East Kilbride, however, is the incidence of good-quality, if sometimes ordinary, buildings of all kinds for the community through to employment purposes. These encompass leisure facilities, major office developments, fast-food outlets, pubs and restaurants and, of course, the many churches.

Urban Sculpture

Urban sculpture also has become an important part of the visual life of the town, from older pieces in the town centre to the mischievous pieces on the Stewartfield Way roundabouts, and the major statement vertical stainless steel 'markers' at the main entrances to the town, and in the principal industrial areas. The Corporation has both commissioned works from local artists and employed a Town Artist. In the 1980s an

Water lilies turned to 'stone' at Calderglen Country Park

Is it a light fitting? Sculpture on the roundabout at the entrance to Centre One, Stewartfield Way

A touch of 'steam and wheels' at the junction of Stewartfield Way and Stewartfield Crescent

important arts project was established with joint funding between the Corporation, the District Council and the Scottish Arts Council. Fiona Dean was the last of a number of artists-in-residence employed under this scheme.

THE HOUSING

Public-sector housing in East Kilbride has never been significantly different from the architecture, design and layout that was contemporary with it. Housing in the town has generally not been about innovation but, at its best, simply being better done than other contemporary housing.

In the early years it was very close in form to the housing being built in some of the contemporary English New Towns, different only in the Scottish idiom of render and roughcast, and the use of walk-up blocks of flats.

No children, but an attractive play area at Stewartfield Loch

Some of the housing in the East and West Mains areas, for instance, and in the Murray, is very good, not only in terms of its own times, but has also matured into an altogether satisfactory and sustainable environment for the 1990s. The 1960s and 1970s avoided over-'fashionable' design and continued to produce ordinary, good-quality homes for an expanding population. Only during the later 1970s and early 1980s is it possible to see in Greenhills that the thoroughness which had characterised so much residential development had been largely exhausted. Even here, however, there are pockets of excellence.

Private housing on the southern edge in Mulberry Drive, Greenhills

Stewartfield, however, goes some way towards redressing the balance, where during its later years the private housing developments have demonstrated a resurgence of enthusiasm by the Development Corporation. Partnerships between

Private housing renaissance in Stewartfield Crescent looking north to Stewartfield Loch

Stepping up the hill: Aikman Place, Calderwood Road

builders and an enlightened developer - the Corporation - have produced an area of quite different ethos to much of the rest of the town - even having regard to some very good earlier private developments.

STEWARTFIELD AND PEEL PARK

The private housing in Stewartfield forms the northern edge of the town, and the principal distributor road, Stewartfield Way, is largely developed only on its southern side. Beyond the road on the north the countryside rises to a near horizon acting as a backdrop to the housing and other developments.

The private housing itself ranges from high-quality detached courts to hard edge - and sometimes mean - terraces. Stewartfield Crescent, a loop off Stewartfield Way, and with a direct link via Stewartfield Road to the town centre and railway station, is a single-carriageway distributor with surface pedestrian crossings and high-quality landscape. There is a rich variety of spring and autumn colours, and green channels following the principal pedestrian routes through the residential areas - even incidental sculpture and generous children's play and kickabout spaces.

North of Stewartfield Way is the recently created Stewartfield Loch adjacent to the historic sixteenth-century Mains Castle tower house. The Loch itself is at the heart of a heritage park and water sports facility with a fine boathouse and a good children's play area. Again, there is the strategic siting of good sculpture by Fiona Dean.

West of Kittoch Water the development is commercial and the ring road changes its name, first to Peel Park Way, and then Redwood Drive, with an important junction with Paisley Road which becomes one of the principal 'gateways' to the town.

'A place of our own' in Burnett Rose Place, off Stewartfield Crescent

'Executive' style in Strathnairn Drive

Stewartfield Loch with the new boating centre and the rather older Mains Castle tower house

A new home for the Tax People at Centre One, Peel Park

This is the Philipshill roundabout and is marked with a colossal stainless steel 'boundary' sculpture, illuminated at night.

Adjacent to this junction is the new home for the Inland Revenue, the new 'Centre One'. Whereas the town centre office was a 'tower', this new creation is a skilful presentation of a very large building. Formed of many parts, planes and surfaces, it deceives the observer into seeing it as smaller than it really is. There is an abiding impression of curved brown facing brick panels, glass, and a juxtaposition of pitched roofs, clerestorey glazing and turrets of glass. Opposite to it is the Stakis Hotel in the 'fat cottage' style - so successful that it has already had to be extended.

INDUSTRY

The Peel Park Campus provides the town with an expanding Science Park. Notable for the Scottish Nuclear HQ - a glazed pagoda with floating roof - set in articulate ground-moulded landscape and entered past an ornamental loch, complete with reed beds and sculptured fountain. The Peel Park Campus, with its growing range of well-designed industrial facilities within a parkland setting, is born of the realisation that successful industrial innovation, crucial to the economic and social well-being of the town, is now dependent upon high-quality design, landscape, layout and materials, if it is to compete in the world of inward investment.

Scottish Nuclear HQ with ornamental pond at Peel Park

It is an area of activity in which East Kilbride has been highly successful, creating in all some 33,000 jobs. Along the way it has created high-quality industrial landscapes, some now more 'dated' than others. Thus there has been the Kelvin Estate and Motorola, Nerston and Rolls-Royce, and the National Engineering Laboratory now translated into the

Rolls-Royce live here: Nerston Industrial Estate

Factory in the trees at Redwood Court

Scottish Enterprise Technology Park by the Birniehill roundabout.

Following initial difficulties with the Scottish Office over funding for 'advance' factories, East Kilbride has pioneered a variety of pre-built standard factories and workshops. It has also been pre-eminent in attracting high-quality investment into the purpose-built plant. Perhaps never mould-breaking in terms of design until Peel Park, it has nevertheless set standards to which others aspired. It has a solid industrial base upon which to build and to continue to contribute to the sustainability of the community and town itself. It has also now established the habit of good design as an essential ingredient of a successful industrial policy. It is to be hoped that those who continue the work of the departed Development Corporation also learn this lesson.

Red and black chequerboard factory at Peel Park

SUMMARY

Scotland's oldest and 'first' New Town has now achieved the status of being the acceptable face of a 'new' community. It has, however, not always been easy, despite the Government steering major State-owned employers towards it during its early years.

In 1975, for instance, the new Strathclyde Regional Council was concerned to see that available inward investment should be directed towards the 'renewal' areas of the City of Glasgow, rather than incurring infrastructure expenditure from a limited public purse in what they saw as the already prosperous new towns of East Kilbride and Cumbernauld. In the course of time the Scottish Office accepted that in reality the alternative to a Scottish New Town was often a town in Eire or Portugal or wherever. Such investment could not be commanded - fair or unfair. So East Kilbride has continued its successful business odyssey for another twenty years.

That odyssey is far from complete.

Chapter Three
GLENROTHES — *The Heart of a Kingdom*

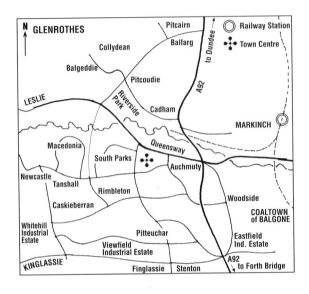

GLENROTHES

Pitcairn	◎ Railway Station
Balfarg	✛ Town Centre
Collydean	
Balgeddie	
Pitcoudie	
LESLIE / Riverside Park	
Cadham	MARKINCH ◎
Macedonia	Queensway
South Parks	Auchmuty
Newcastle	
Tanshall	
Rimbleton	
Caskieberran	Woodside
	COALTOWN of BALGONE
Whitehill Industrial Estate	Pitteuchar	Eastfield Ind. Estate
Viewfield Industrial Estate	
KINGLASSIE	Finglassie	Stenton	A92 to Forth Bridge

- *Location* : Fife

- *Designated* : 1948

- *Area* : 5730 acres

- *Population* : 40,000

Not a war memorial, but a 'boundary marker' for Glenrothes from the south at the Bankhead Interchange

INTRODUCTION

Glenrothes is neat, manicured and well maintained. Sharing with East Kilbride a 1940s 'designation' it is less well known than its western twin. Forty thousand people now live there, but the people of Glenrothes have had to fight hard over almost 50 years to create the modest and prosperous town which is now theirs.

A town of many surprises, it commands a fierce loyalty from its citizens. In many ways it is the beating heart of the Kingdom of Fife.

THE LOCATION

Glenrothes lies in central Fife at the northern edge of the traditional industrial heartland of the Kingdom, and separated from the agricultural north by the East Lomond Hill.

It lies on a historic route to the north, from Kirkcaldy on the Forth to the ferries to Dundee on the Tay. This route passes through a barrier of low hills at New Inn to enter the rich lands of the Howe of Fife. Cupar, the historic county town of Fife, is 12 miles away and Dundee over the Tay Road Bridge, 27 miles. Whereas the traffic that passes this way in bygone ages had come over the Forth by ferry, travellers from the south and west now come to Glenrothes by the A92 from the M90 and the Forth Road Bridge - 17 miles away. The main east coast railway

The town centre glimpsed through mature landscape, Cadham

from Edinburgh to Aberdeen follows this same route north, with a station at Markinch.

Lying just north of the coal-bearing stratas of central Fife, the site of Glenrothes is bounded by the small towns of Leslie and Kinglassie to the west, Markinch and Coaltown of Balgonie to the east, and Thornton to the south. The designated area is bisected from west to east by the river Leven and the picturesque valley within which it runs.

The Leven Bridge carrying the Western Distributor launches itself over the valley of the river Leven

THE STORY

National energy strategy was the motivating factor in the designation of Glenrothes. The will to live has been the trigger for its development. Post-war Britain needed energy to drive its industrial recovery. This need, married to political ideology, went hand in hand with the nationalisation of the coal industry. In Scotland the Lanarkshire coalfields were in decline, and in strategic terms the coalfields of the Lothians and Fife were seen as an important resource to be developed.

Crocodiles invade Pitcoudie!

The reserves of coal around Thornton to the south of what is now Glenrothes had long been known to be there. A programme of bores demonstrated them to be extensive and preparations were made for their exploitation. The Fife Coal Company began the process towards development, and this was taken over by the new National Coal Board at nationalisation on 1 January 1947. The reserves were to be exploited from a new colliery - the Rothes - to be sited to the west of Thornton and lying on the railway loop from Dunfermline. In 1947 two large concrete winding gear towers were built, dominating the landscape for many miles around.

Terrace in Pitcoudie

It was thought that the Rothes would employ some 2500 miners as part of 6500 new mining jobs coming to the Fife coalfield. Many of these miners and their families were to come

Private bungalows in John Knox Gardens, Pitcairn

'A 19th-century public house which wasn't there yesterday': the Fettykil Fox in Leslie Road

The town centre 'towers' seen from the west along Leslie Road

to Fife from Lanarkshire in the west of Scotland. They were in part to be housed within the existing surrounding communities, but 3500 of them were to be located within a New Town to be built in the area. This was the motive behind the proposals in the plan prepared by Sir Frank Mears for the Scottish Office, and published in 1946.

A New Town in central Fife therefore had a clear place in national policy terms. It had the support of the Labour Government and of Fife County Council. There were disputes, however, as to both its precise location and its name.

For its location, consideration was given to siting the town around an existing centre - Markinch, in particular. This was discounted because of the limitations of the centre of Markinch itself. It would, however, have allowed the development of the railway station at Markinch to serve it. In due course all the adjacent towns - Leslie, Kinglassie, Coaltown and Markinch - made it known that they preferred to be left out of the designated area of the New Town. Ironically, all now sit on the periphery of Glenrothes and are in part surrounded by it. Their lives are dominated by the economic and social life of their larger neighbour.

The eventual site was some 5730 acres of 'great natural beauty astride the river Leven between Markinch and Leslie'. There was already a paper-making industry in this valley, at the Tullis Russell Mills in the east and at the Fettykil Mills in the west.

These paper-makers along with the agricultural interests objected to the Designation Order when it was published by the Secretary of State in January 1948. They failed, however, to persuade the subsequent Public Inquiry, and Glenrothes was

Crowded to the edge: betting shop, built when the town centre was empty, and now almost engulfed in the multi-deck car park

North Street, town centre, with Glenrothes House on left

formally designated on 30 June 1948. The population was to be 32,000.

One of the ironies of the eventual success of Glenrothes was that when in due course it was granted Special Development Status under the then Industry Act, Smith Anderson at Fettykil Mills were to find themselves outside the Designated Area, and thus 'outside' the *largesse* from which the town benefited.

The issue of the name was disputed almost as keenly as the site of the town. The name Rothes had been suggested, but was objected to on the grounds that there was already a Rothes in Moray. Some people felt anyway that it should be named 'Westwood' after Joseph Westwood MP who was not only the Secretary of State for Scotland and an ardent supporter of the New Town, but also a miner and a Fifer. Fife County Council, however, narrowly supported the name Glenrothes, and this in due course it became, although not before the Secretary of State had indicated that he believed that it should be Balgonie.

The first Chairman of the Development Corporation Board was Sir Hector McNeill, a former Lord Provost of Glasgow. John Sneddon from Kelty, the County Convener, was Vice-Chairman, and the legendary J.M.Mitchell, the County Clerk, was also to be a Board member. This heralded a long association between the Development Corporation and the County Council and its successors, which brought many of the county's finest servants into membership of the Board, e.g. Sir George Sharp, County and Region Convener and Convener of COSLA (Convention of Scottish Local Authorities), Robert Gough, Region Convener for 18 years, and Elizabeth Henderson, councillor and tireless worker for the Glenrothes community.

Murchison Path, Collydean

Housing facing onto the Balfarg Henge

'A traditional approach': Alan McLure House - a residential home, Balbirnie Road, Woodside

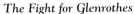

Once the Auchmuty Centre, now a part of the town centre

Glenrothes was also to share with East Kilbride the distinction of a 'common' Chairman with another New Town. This was Lord Hughes of Hawkhill, a former Lord Provost of Dundee who was the Chairman of the Glenrothes Board from 1960 to 1964, and Chairman of the East Kilbride Board from 1975 to 1982. During the period between he held various portfolios as a Scottish Office Minister.

The Glenrothes Board's first meeting was held in Edinburgh on 5 November 1948 at St Andrew's House. Before the formal business began the meeting was addressed by the Secretary of State, Arthur Woodburn MP, in much the same manner as the first meeting of the East Kilbride Board had been addressed by Joseph Westwood. Sadly, Westwood had been killed in a motor car accident before this event was to take place.

The first General Manager was Frank Preston, Burgh Surveyor of Milngavie. The Chief Architect was E.A.Ferriby, followed soon by the better-known Peter Tinto. A legal assistant to J.M.Mitchell in the County Offices, Jim Roger became Secretary and Legal Adviser. Jim Young was the first Finance Officer. It was to be 1952 before the first tenants were allocated houses planned and built by the Development Corporation.

The Fight for Glenrothes

Glenrothes, however, had still to face a crisis of confidence which was of such proportions that the town's survival of it was to shape both it and its people for generations to come. Glenrothes was never intended to be a 'coal town' in the sense of being a single-industry community. Coal-miners were never to be more than a one-in-six component part of the working

The Standing Stones, Colliston Avenue, Pitteuchar

population. Like the other post-war New Towns it was to be a balanced community, and that meant attracting other kinds of employment to the town. Like East Kilbride, however, Glenrothes was to have serious and lengthy disagreement with the Scottish Office over the funding and building of 'advance' factories to attract a balance of employment to the town.

The failure to achieve this, allied to the slower than anticipated build-up of the mining population, led to the Secretary of State announcing in 1955 a partial stoppage of the development. This was done in a press release and a letter to the County Council, stating that house building was to be halted, allowing only the existing housing contracts to be completed. Continued development was to wait until the creation of employment in the Rothes Pit caught up with the existing provision. In the run-up to this decision the target population had already been diminished from 32,000 to 15,000 people. The scene for conflict was thus set.

Post-and-stay footbridge carries pedestrians over Western Avenue between Pitcoudie and Pitcairn

Complementary to the objections of the Development Corporation Board, this 'Fight for Glenrothes' was in large part a community-led affair. It brought a number of activists to the fore who were to go on to be the civic leaders in Fife in the next generation - men such as Bob King, later the long-serving Provost of Kirkcaldy District Council; Alan McLure, who went on to be the leader of Fife Regional Council; and Alex Devlin, long-serving Education Convener. The 'Fight for Glenrothes' was also in a sense the precursor to the later 'Fight for Fife', when the Government of two decades later tried to divide Fife as a part of the Local Government restructuring of 1975.

Back in 1955, however, production at the Rothes Pit was not expected to start until 1956, and in the event was delayed until 1957. By 1956 there were suggestions of some Glasgow

Simple dignity: St Margaret's Church of Scotland, Woodside Road

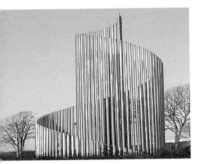

Swirling 'organ pipes' on a roundabout at Westwood Park

The A92 crosses over Woodside Road in the only grade-separated crossing - but no junction

'overspill', and the attraction of industry to the town was at least sufficiently successful as to allow some relaxation of the Scottish Office's building restrictions. By 1957 an 'overspill' agreement was entered into with Glasgow under the provisions of the Housing & Town Development (Scotland) Order 1957, but was never to result in any significant transfer of population under its provisions. The fight was on its way to being won!

Other significant developments were taking place on the industrial front. Beckman Instruments came to the Queensway Industrial Estate (and are still there) - this was the beginning of a place for Glenrothes in 'Silicon Glen'. Other industries followed, amongst them Anderson Boyes (later Anderson Strathclyde), which made components for coal-cutting machinery.

The 'Fight for Glenrothes' was successful, but the town could have been stillborn. The relationships formed, however, led directly to a bond between town and county, which was in due course to place Glenrothes at the heart of the Kingdom of Fife.

The Rothes Pit

The Rothes eventually came on stream in June 1957, and in the same year the Thornton railway marshalling yard was opened - the most modern in Britain. Both Glenrothes and its adjacent coalmine were indeed at the 'cutting edge' of technologies, both old and new. The Rothes, however, was destined never to employ more than about 800 miners. It suffered first from a revision of the Government's Energy Policy in 1959, with an acknowledgement that there was a reduced national demand for coal. There was to be a reduction in output of coal from the Rothes, and a consequent reduction in

The town centre turns its back on the Leven Valley - the backs of the
Fife House offices

the number of miners coming to Fife from the west of Scotland
- King Coal was dying. Quite apart, however, from the national
scene, the Rothes had problems with both faulted seams and
flooding, both of which contributed to expensive working.
By 1961, just four years after production started, the Rothes
was dead.

The threat to Glenrothes could have been devastating. The
'fight' of the mid-1950s, however, had not been in vain.
Glenrothes was no longer dependent upon King Coal.

The Rothes closed, leaving behind it the empty concrete
winding towers - tombstones to the dying of a way of life
in Fife.

A Footnote

No account of the development of Glenrothes can be complete
without a reference in passing to the infamous 'Cadco Affair'.
This was a grandiose scheme to develop a large food-processing
facility at Queensway, with an associated piggery at Whitehill
for 20,000 pigs. The film star, George Saunders, was associated
with the Cadco Company, and his name lent credibility to the
proposals. There was even to be a film studio! Appearing on
the scene in 1963, at a time when Glenrothes was still a
vulnerable place, Cadco collapsed financially within two years,
leaving considerable hurt and distress behind. All the Cadco
buildings, however, were soon to see new use as advance
factories. (The Glenrothes 'pig factory' became a cautionary
tale told around the other Scottish New Towns.)

Glenrothes Reborn

The 1960s then became a period of resourceful if slow action
for the future of the town. The town centre itself reflected

'Chamber' offices in brick at Hanover
Court, with Fife House glimpsed in the
background

Major pedestrian and cycle route passes under Woodside Road

the dilemma. The first phase of the shopping centre located at the Auchmuty end of the central area was a gaunt square with a three-storey-high glazed shed roof, partially open at the sides. Opened in 1961 it sat on the eastern edge of a very large open space. There was little else which could be called a town centre.

By 1975, however, the central role of Glenrothes in the hearts of the people of Fife was demonstrated by the new Fife Regional Council locating its headquarters in the town rather than in the county town of Cupar. Over the next decade virtually all the principal functions of the Council had been located in Glenrothes. In 1996 this was followed by the new unitary authority - Fife Council - making the same decision. In a very real sense, Glenrothes was now the centre of Fife.

That the Development Corporation resisted the temptation for inappropriate development in the central area over more than a decade of waiting is testimony to their determination to see the town grow properly, even if slowly. From that first draughty shed to the opening of the fourth phase of the fully enclosed and indoor shopping centre three decades were to elapse. New Towns were designated in hope. Glenrothes demonstrates that eventually they must be won by their patient people.

'Politely suburban': Collydean Primary School

The Plan

The outline plan of 1951 shows a New Town similar to others of the time, with the principal roads linking the town with its neighbours north south and east west, and a system of distributor roads linking the residential and industrial areas. All the junctions of roads are at 'grade'. It was different in detail from the preliminary plan prepared by the Scottish Office, but similar in kind.

Obelisk and flowers mark the entrance to Viewfield Industrial Estate

Even flat-roofed buildings survive the decades in Glenrothes: police station, town centre

The central area is located on the southern lip of the valley of the river Leven. There was a branch railway from the main line at Markinch westwards to Leslie. This ran as a loop along the southern edges of the proposed town; it seems never to have been considered as a possible transport link for the town centre, and was to be closed by British Railways in 1967, becoming instead a footpath and cycle track. There is also a railway spur into the Leven Valley to serve the Tullis Russell Mills. The unchanged station at Markinch has forlornly proclaimed itself for four decades as the place to 'alight for Glenrothes'. It has now been joined by a change in the name of the station on the Fife loop line at Thornton. This equally distant place is now called 'Glenrothes'! Like most of Scotland, however, if you want public transport in Glenrothes, it is a bus or a taxi.

There are, however, cycle tracks in many places running parallel with the extensive system of pedestrian routes, and this has now been recognised by the Millennium Commission in the granting of funding for the improvement of these, the provision of cycle tracks alongside roads and protected road-crossing points. It is anticipated that in due course the Glenrothes routes will link up with a network of cycle-ways throughout Fife.

The master plan for the town, however, was not a revolution, even for 1951. It has changed only to the degree of recognising the changes in the northern part of the designated area and establishing the western distributor road. The plan is to be applauded therefore for its consistency.

THE TOWN CENTRE

The central area of Glenrothes lies where it was planned to be more than four decades ago, on the southern rim of

A 'folly' to mark the Kingdom Centre

The eastern Albany Gate pedestrian entrance to the Kingdom Centre

The western 'pedestrian versus motor cars' entrance to the Kingdom Centre

the valley of the River Leven; but it has been denied the imaginative link to that picturesque valley and Riverside Park which might well have seemed to be appropriate. It is a modest centre, now largely complete, which has progressed incrementally over the life of the town.

The Kingdom Centre

The shopping centre itself began on the assumption that, like its English counterparts, it would have open-air pedestrian shopping squares and streets. In the event, the shopping areas have always been in covered malls. The problems over the future of the town in the 1950s meant that it was 1961 before work began on the first phase of shops, in what is now Lyon Square. This was capped by a vast three-storey-high glazed roof which was partially open at the sides; a 'neither fish nor fowl' solution which determined the designers that Glenrothes would have a totally enclosed, environmentally controlled, shopping centre. In the meantime, a three-storey Co-operative Department Store was added at the eastern entrance, but it was to be another twelve years before the next phase of the centre was built.

The 'mini Crystal Palace' interior of the bus station access to the Kingdom Centre

The distinctive Clock Tower by what is now the Albany Gate was donated by a former Chairman of the Development Corporation, Sir Garnett Wilson, at the time of the opening of the first phase. This clock together with the shops mentioned and the Golden Acorn Hotel (now the Albany) give the eastern entrance to the Kingdom Centre its still distinctive 'southern' New Town feel.

With all four phases of the Kingdom Centre now complete Glenrothes possesses a competent and comfortable centre which is both adequate to its needs, and to those of the smaller communities around it.

The Kingdom Centre Malls

Lyon Square, once the hub of much of the communal life of Glenrothes, and of a spectacular water feature sculpture, is now roofed at the fascia height of its surrounding shops. The effect is gloomy, and not much relieved by the roof lights which cast a modest highlight on a café corral, jaunty stalls on wheels, regimented banners and a well-patterned floor. The hub of activity has moved away to the west of the centre. Lyon Way, leading gently uphill from it to the Falkland Gate, is cheerful and usually well crowded with people walking between the bus station and the newer parts of the centre.

Unicorn Square lacks vitality and interest, despite being at one of the main access points to the centre. It is currently home to Malcolm Robertson's *Seated Old Couple*, 1979, in bronze, frequently joined by passing children. The natural light is subdued, however, by the effect of the 'yellowing' of the acrylic dome. From there Unicorn Way again rises gently to meet the gleaming daylit malls of the fourth phase - the contrast with the older malls is dramatic.

The 'grand' floor design in the fourth-phase Kingdom Centre mall, with its brass medallions of the 'Families of Fife'

There is height, and there is light. The surfaces are light. The banners march on, but they lead to a crowning glory which is beneath the feet of the visitor. The star-shaped floor design with its bronze medallions is the focus of the two-storey square at the entrance to the Rothes Halls. Even if the internal landscape is dull, this active square rises to have at least a hint of the 'winter garden' which the then Chief Architect, Sandy Bannerman, envisaged, but the Corporation couldn't fully afford.

The 'Winter Garden' entrance to the Rothes Halls from the Kingdom Centre mall

Fife House, old and new - the original was built by the Development Corporation for their own use; the 'shiny extension' by Fife Regional Council

The public entrance to the headquarters of Fife Council in Fife House

The Wider Centre

There is much more, however, to the town centre of Glenrothes than its ever so slowly evolving shopping centre. The town has enjoyed the commitment of the 'official' community of wider Fife, and this is now to be seen in the 'developer' office blocks containing the many departments of Fife Council. The Regional Council, Fife Health Board and the Development Corporation itself have all passed this way, and in doing so injected employment and purchasing power into the place.

Some, like the 'Lubianka'-style Rothesay House - see it on a wet day - were built speculatively for the Regional Council to lease, and in due course purchase. Fife House, in its dark black concrete panels and vertical white stripes, was built by the Corporation for itself, and vacated by them in 1975 to win the Region to their town. Its shiny metal and green plastic extension, complete with brick clock tower, was the work of the Regional Council itself. The rustic brick of the Kingdom House brought 'chambers' and yellow brick sheltered internal courtyards to office development.

North Street has recently been cut in two and a new pedestrian square of patterned brick paviors created.

'Concrete panel developer' offices at Rothesay House, town centre

Well-landscaped car park off North Street, town centre

Simple brick dignity for the Social Work Office, town centre

St Columba's Church of Scotland marks the south-west corner of the town centre

At the western end of the centre St Columba's Parish Church brings another punctuating point with its triangular roof and framed stark bell tower. The adjoining Social Work Office is almost Georgian in its brown brick and domestic formality.

The Glenrothes town centre reflects the story of the town. It is far from pretentious, but is quietly successful. It provides shopping and commercial activity, along with facilities such as cinema and ten-pin bowling, pubs, restaurants, hotel, bookies and bingo. It is actually a very pleasing place to be in. Its most public and familiar face being the Benno Schotz statue *Ex Terra*, 1965 - a mother with her six children - 25 feet high at the bus station entrance to the Kingdom Centre. Commissioned by the Corporation and unveiled in 1965, its surroundings have changed beyond recognition. Such is the pace of things, even in towns where they happen slowly.

The *Ex Terra* sculpture by Benno Schotz fronts the 'conservatory' bus station

The Glenrothes centre, however, has, like East Kilbride, spilled beyond the bounds set for it by the master plan. A site to the east of the present centre, once occupied by the now relocated Beckmans and long-gone Anderson Strathclyde, has become a Retail Park. Well, at least it has a supermarket in a 1930s 'airport' style, and a filling station, and also the standard McDonald's Restaurant. Work is seen also to be proceeding upon a bingo hall.

McDonald's Restaurant comes to Glenrothes at the retail park, Queensway

TOWNSCAPE

Topography

The designated area is divided east/west by the Leven Valley. Between its indigenous paper mills this now contains the Riverside Park - a delightful lung which allows the town to breathe and is well used by its residents. Woodland, trees and

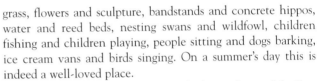

A sunny summer Sunday afternoon in Riverside Park

Trees, grass, sculpture and anonymous terraces in Newcastle

Flowers for Robert Burns at South Parks

Sold for £1000: Balbirnie House Hotel in Balbirnie Park - home in the past to the Development Corporation

grass, flowers and sculpture, bandstands and concrete hippos, water and reed beds, nesting swans and wildfowl, children fishing and children playing, people sitting and dogs barking, ice cream vans and birds singing. On a summer's day this is indeed a well-loved place.

To the north the ground rises to the lower slopes of the East Lomond Hill. To the south it rises steeply out of the valley and then gently to a low rounded ridge, and to another, before dipping gently to the coal-bearing plain towards Kirkcaldy on the Firth of Forth.

Townscape

The ambience of Glenrothes is a tapestry of low brown roofs, mostly pitched, and set amongst the foliage of ample trees. There are trees on the internal skylines and woodland reaches in fingers along the pedestrian routes to the town centre. The town is in the happy situation that much of its tree and shrub planting is nearing maturity, giving it a containment - a kind of eastern 'dear green place' - and colour in both leaf and flower. Open space is ample. Like East Kilbride, Glenrothes has generous playing fields and parkland.

The 'stately home' of Balbirnie House, once the very grand headquarters of the Corporation, is now an exclusive hotel. Its parkland, however, lying between the town and Markinch, provides not only a high-quality and much-used open space, but also a backdrop to the higher-quality private housing being developed here.

Building in Glenrothes is largely domestic in scale until the town centre is reached. Only here are there higher structures which punctuate the profile of the town, and on an almost American model say, 'This is the middle - you can see it -

Raeburn Heights, the town's only tower block, marks the entrance to the town centre, seen down Rothes Road

drive/walk towards it and you will find it.' You almost always do!

The colour palette for the buildings is always restrained. Greys, and browns, and shades of both. Some red, some green, plenty of Scottish harling, but more brown bricks in the early days than you would expect. North of the Leven the brown houses creep up the slopes in luxuriant landscape, until they meet the trim gardens of the 'developer' private houses on their narrow plots.

Brown housing in Cadham, to the north of the town centre

There are not many dramatic townscape features in Glenrothes; but 1996 saw the opening of the Leven Bridge carrying the Western Distributor Road over the valley of the river Leven. This bold expression of bridge engineering was designed by the Babtie Group for the outgoing Development Corporation. A priceless bequest to the town, its soaring road deck is suspended from a gleaming white tower by black cables. The tower is a landmark on the western approaches from Leslie.

Landscape

Landscape within the older neighbours is now rich and mature. There is a heavy dependence in the earlier areas on mown grass and on urban trees. This means that often the quite ordinary surrounding housing is lent mystery by only being glimpsed through foliage as the observer moves past. On the south-facing lower slopes of the East Lomond Hill the shrub and tree planting is richly mature, giving in some cases the feeling that the houses are about to be engulfed in leaf and green.

Glenrothes has always placed great stress on its roundabouts, with the planting out in season of a sea of colour

Housing lost in trees, off South Parks Road

South Parks Road leads towards the town centre

Mature landscape in Alexander Road, Auchmuty

Saltire Centre Offices in Pentland Park

Pedestrian routes and housing, Cadham

The Fife Institute: Sports Centre and Swimming Pool - part of the County Council's dowry to the town

- mostly red. Major open spaces are extensive and almost all grassed and neatly mown in season, with parkland trees. The principal and distributor roads all have a good depth of associated landscaping, which means that driving around the town creates the impression of a very 'green' place. Perhaps the industrial areas are more minimal in their approach, but there is carefully sited tree planting which gives maximum impact for minimum input, although the Saltire Centre is an exception in that a rich and coloured landscape has been seen as a part of the attraction for inward investment there.

The Neighbourhood Centres

For many years the Woodside Centre, pedestrian square, flats over shops, trees, paving and sculpture, was the effective town centre of the older parts of the town. As good a village atmosphere exists today as when it was opened by HM The Queen in 1958.

The Glamis Centre, by contrast, is a rather thin 1960s thing with flat roofs instead of flats. Leading into one of the best underpasses in the town it also contains a public house. The Cadham Centre belongs to that later era of brown bricks and brown paviors. Well mannered and maintained, it is contained by a matching set of buildings embracing offices, pub, neighbourhood centre and Christ's Kirk on the Hill with its tiny 'needle' steeple.

Other Buildings

Fife County Council and Fife Regional Council invested heavily and imaginatively in Glenrothes. There are secondary schools which were at the forefront in design in their time, immaculate primary and nursery schools, and much else. It was in the provision of a major sports facility at the Fife Institute and at the Glenrothes College, however, that this endowment of the town is to be seen at its best, carefully nurtured and extended facilities which have both enhanced the town socially and physically.

These are, in a sense, only the 'tip of an iceberg' of good-quality provision from a variety of sources.

Glenrothes College: part of the County Council's dedication to good education facilities

Urban Sculpture

Glenrothes is scattered with urban sculpture, *Ex Terra* being among the earliest. A town artist, David Harding, was appointed in 1968 and held the position for ten years. He was assisted by Stanley Bonnar. They produced incidental pipes and tables and so on in all sorts of places. There are marching hippos, threatening crocodiles, toadstools, chariots, henges, people, and much else - all serving to add a dimension of visual diversity to the townscape of the place.

Harding was followed by Malcolm Robertson. It was he who created the 'giant lilies' for the Glasgow Garden Festival in 1988. Returned to the town at the close of the Festival they now grace the junction of Leslie Road and Western Avenue. Robertson's most famous work is the life-size bronze of dancing children to the south of the town centre; called *The Dream*, its children are 'dancing for a united world'.

'Poor man's Corbusier': St Paul's RC Church

The very improbable *Giant Lilies* by Malcolm Robertson on Leslie Road - made for the Glasgow Garden Festival

The timeless dance of children playing in bronze - *The Dream* by Malcolm Robertson in Church Street, south of the town centre

The Defenceless One by Rudolf Christian Baischi broods over Riverside Park

The Riverside Park contains two important works bound up with the civic life of the Town. *The Defenceless One* is a brooding bronze figure by Rudolf Christian Baischi, presented to Glenrothes by its twin town, Boblingen, in 1991. Nearby is *The Good Samaritan* by Donald Rae in a yellow stone, commissioned by the Corporation to mark the town's fortieth birthday in 1988, and unveiled by HRH The Prince of Wales.

HOUSING

Much has been said already about the housing in the town. In the early days of the town it shared with East Kilbride the knack of doing the normal very well. A presumption against joining in the fashions of the day has meant that there is only a single multi-storey block of flats in the town, and that is mercifully adjacent to the town centre and other high buildings. For the rest, it is a combination of terraces and courts, a small number of low-rise flats and a careful use of building form to create enclosure.

Only once did Glenrothes reluctantly stray far, when it accepted its share of Jesperson 'walk-up' maisonettes and flats. These are located in Caskieberran and are in much their original form. They are rescued by the quality of landscaping around them.

Sadly fashion and cost also dictated flat roofs in parts of Pitteuchar and Macedonia. They are the only real failure in Glenrothes on the housing front.

Cadham and Pitcoudie brought a change in style, with staggered terraces clawing their way up the hillsides. Brown and mono-pitched, with some of the finest pedestrian ways in any of the Scottish New Towns, rich in drama and foliage, light and shade. Safe and sheltered places for children

St Margaret's Drive, Auchmuty, with the town centre in the background

Dunbeath Drive, Pitteuchar

Early housing in Lomond Way, Woodside

on sunny summer days. Then it is onto the private dreams of another generation of Glenrothes citizens: the well-mannered estates of private housing looking out over the town from the Lomond foothills.

INDUSTRY

There are few flights of architectural achievement in the Glenrothes Industrial Estates, but a great many workmanlike places of employment, generally all well maintained and neat. Only the Saltire Centre brings the high-tech face of high-quality design as a means of supporting employment. Now after the demise of the Development Corporation, Fife Enterprise are building good-quality factories at Westwood Park on the southern edge of Glenrothes.

SUMMARY

Glenrothes has never been a dramatic place, and its growth has been slow. During the 1950s its very future seemed really to be in doubt. It has, however, become a very satisfactory town. It demonstrates that even in New Towns the best results are achieved by a careful incremental growth, rather than a short time-scale of equal-age development.

Like any long-standing community, however, it now finds itself threatened by the presence of larger neighbours. A major Retail Park complete with Sainsbury and much else is being developed at Chapel Farm to the north of Kirkcaldy and strategically located on the East Fife Regional Road just to the south of Glenrothes.

Glenrothes has developed a very loyal community, and this is evidenced by the care which is extended to the town. There is graffiti in all of Scotland's New Towns; there is, however, only a very little of it in Glenrothes. In the spring a swan sits upon a nest in the Riverside Park within yards of the busy town centre. Its security speaks volumes for this modest place.

Flats in Abbotsford Drive, Caskieberran

Discovery Electronics, Eastfield Industrial Estate

Fife Enterprise still building in Westwood Park Industrial Estate

Children's play area in Parkland, Pitcairn

The 'corporate British eating style': the Bankhead Gate Tavern and Travel Inn

Chapter Four

CUMBERNAULD – *A Flawed Utopia?*

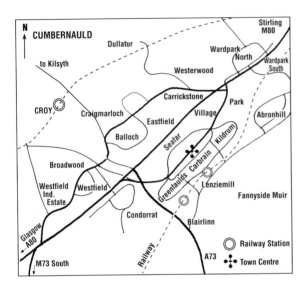

- *Location:* North Lanarkshire

- *Designated:* 1955

- *Area:* 7788 acres

- *Population:* 52,000

Cumbernauld House provided a home for the Development Corporation, and its Park a 'lung' for the people living on the hill

Jane's Brae looking south with Carbrain on the left

INTRODUCTION

Cumbernauld has been visited for decades by planners, architects and social scientists from all over the world. In 1967 the American Institute of Architects awarded its prestigious R.S.Reynolds Memorial Award for Community Architecture to the town. The citation left no doubt that Cumbernauld was viewed internationally as being a very important place:

> Scotland's Cumbernauld is undoubtedly the most comprehensive project of community architecture to date. Rarely has a group of architects and their allied professionals and consultants produced a more carefully developed scheme on this scale. Throughout the project evidence is found of devotion to the overall problem and superb skill in urban design.

Similarly over a period of twenty years from 1961 the Saltire Society made twelve awards and commendations to the town in recognition of good 'Housing Design'.

Yet amidst all of this recognition Cumbernauld has remained an enigma for many Scots. Even today, an admission of residence, or former residence, can elicit vivid reactions and even expressions of sympathy! Perhaps this is because much of Cumbernauld does not resemble earlier New Towns, let alone the modern private housing estate. Perhaps even it is because

The Seafar 'split-level' houses: the best-known face of Cumbernauld

Daffodils provide a spring carpet beneath the 'snake' footbridge between Kildrum and Seafar

there are many people who have only seen it in passing, either speeding along the A80, or passing through the town on buses *en route* to somewhere else.

Cumbernauld, however, is not for those who take an external and superficial view. Cumbernauld is for those who either have the time to explore it, use it, or indeed to live within it. It is a town of immense character and considerable diversity.

THE LOCATION

Cumbernauld lies 13 miles to the north-east of Glasgow astride the A80, the main trunk road to Stirling. The junction of this road with the motorway from the south, the M73, lies on its western boundary. The main Glasgow to Edinburgh railway is on the northern edge of the boundary of the designated area with a station at Croy, whilst the original Cumbernauld station which provides the principal rail link to Glasgow lies to the south. The smaller town of Kilsyth is situated 5 miles to the north.

Red bus passes beneath a footbridge on Greenfaulds Road

THE STORY

Following the designation of East Kilbride in 1947 Glasgow City Council continued with their view that the city's housing problems could be solved within the boundaries of the city. After the General Election of 1951 this view coincided with that of the new Conservative Government under Winston Churchill. This Government was concerned at the increasing cost to the Exchequer of the New Towns already being built. They were not keen to see any more designated under the 1946 Act. They looked rather to 'Town Development' Schemes in which existing communities were to be expanded to receive overspill population from the great cities. In 1952 a Town Development Act was approved by Parliament to facilitate this approach. It did not, however, apply to Scotland. In Parliament

Kildrum Primary School

Kildrum Church of Scotland Parish Church

Pedestrian way from Carbrain into the town centre passes The Tryst Leisure Centre, with Fleming House Offices beyond

the new Secretary of State for Scotland, James Stuart, was questioned about this omission. He replied that there was 'no particular overspill problem in Scotland'.

In that happy way, however, that the convenient and the inconvenient have of coinciding, 1952 was also the year in which A.G.Jury, the new Chief Architect for Glasgow, published a Report 'demonstrating conclusively...that the city could not solve its housing and population problems within its own boundaries'. This was a direct contradiction of the Bruce Report referred to under East Kilbride. In 1953 there was a Public Inquiry into Glasgow's 'Draft Development Plan', at which Glasgow stuck to its original position and even declined to call Archibald Jury to give evidence.

Notwithstanding this position the Secretary of State had by then become sufficiently concerned at the problems facing Glasgow, that he re-convened the defunct Clyde Valley Regional Planning Advisory Committee to urgently consider the problems of Glasgow overspill. By August 1953 this group had produced an interim Report in which they supported the findings of the 1946 Clyde Valley Regional Plan, and demonstrated that there was still an overspill problem of up to 300,000 people. The City of Glasgow was by now inclined to share this opinion. The site at Cumbernauld, first proposed in the 1946 Plan, was to be reactivated as a possible site for a New Town to serve as a destination for overspill population from Glasgow.

A Town at Cumbernauld?

Robert Grieve, Chief Planner at the Scottish Office, made a technical examination of the site and confirmed the location as being satisfactory for a town of 50,000-80,000 people. There

The 'executive' tower blocks in Kildrum have their own multi-deck car park connected by footbridge to the flats - a 1960s excess

Industrial blue glass and trees, Westfield

was some debate as to how the town was to be promoted, with the proposal arising that Glasgow might itself undertake the development, subsuming the site into the city's control, as a sort of detached 'Glasgow in the country'.

In the meantime, however, and in order to demonstrate the scale of the problem, Robert Grieve had conducted a group of Treasury officials around both the site for the town and also some of the worst parts of the overcrowded Glasgow slums. When the Government's approval was finally given, however, it was for a designation under the 1946 New Towns Act - but unlike East Kilbride and Glenrothes, the exporting authority, Glasgow, was to make a financial contribution to the development.

The Draft Designation Order was for a town on a site of 4150 acres of 50,000 people, 85% of whom were to be nominated by Glasgow. After considerable debate between the various parties the city's contribution was to be £140 per house for those whom they nominated tenants, that is £14 per house for a period of 10 years. In the event this arrangement lasted only until 1972.

A 'village street' at High Street, Weavers Brae, Craigmarloch

The Town is Designated

The subsequent Public Inquiry lasted for only one day, and the Designation Order was published on 9 December 1955. The designation of Cumbernauld was notable not only for being the first New Town of the 1950s in Britain, but also the last. A proposal by the Greater London Council to build a town at Hook was never implemented.

The designated area was wholly contained within what was then the 'separated' eastern part of Dunbartonshire. The industrial area at Blairlinn by the village of Luggiebank in

Pedestrian bridge over Blackthorn Road adjacent to the Abronhill Centre

A pedestrian street of a closed-in kind, Maclehose Road, Kildrum

Footbridge at 'Langlands/Seafar' leads to the town centre

Lanarkshire was not included within the area until 1959. The villages of Condorrat in the west, and Cumbernauld in the east, were included from the beginning, making them an integral part of the development of the town, unlike Leslie and Markinch in relation to Glenrothes.

The Development Corporation

The Development Corporation held its first meeting on 2 March 1956. The first Chairman was General Sir Gordon MacMillan. There were also representatives of Glasgow Corporation, Dunbarton County Council and Cumbernauld District Council. This first meeting was attended by, amongst others, Robert Grieve, who drew attention to the fact that as a consequence of a 50,000 population on what was a relatively small and difficult site, the housing densities would be some 60% higher than the older New Towns.

The die was cast. Cumbernauld was to be a very different place from the New Towns which had gone before. This was, in part, a reaction against what by then was being perceived by many people as a lack of any proper 'urban' feel to the older 'Garden City' New Towns.

The first General Manager was G.R.B. McGill - a man whose impeccable Scottish local government background was to prove to be a perfect balance to the very different team of creative design professionals who were then assembled. Jim Young, Finance Officer in Glenrothes, joined Roy McGill to fulfil the same function in Cumbernauld. He was later joined by his colleague Jim Roger to become Secretary & Legal Adviser.

Pedestrian way seen from an underpass beneath Seafar Road

The Designers

The first Chief Architect and Planning Officer was Hugh Wilson who, although having no direct New Town experience, was convinced of the need for higher-density solutions. His previous appointment had been in Canterbury. He built up a multi-disciplinary team drawn from all over Britain and abroad. This team worked in multi-professional design groups, and in the first years all the professions worked under his direction. The early days of the team were 'heady times' for those involved. There was a rare atmosphere of pioneering adventure. Those involved believed themselves to be engaged upon something new, something unique. Whatever the outcome, they were to be marked for the rest of their careers. They had been in Cumbernauld!

THE PLAN

Although the Scottish Office officials had prepared their own plan for Cumbernauld, in much the same way as had been done for East Kilbride and Glenrothes, Hugh Wilson's team set about doing their own thing. From the beginning, however, the team faced a challenge beyond that faced by its predecessors in the earlier New Towns - the topography of the site. The results were to be regarded as mould-breaking.

The Topography

The designated area was small. Not all of it was buildable, anyway. Its centre was a long hilltop ridge at some 500 feet above sea-level, to the north and south of which were valleys. The hill itself had steep north-facing slopes and gentler south-facing. To the south-east the Red Burn flowed out through woodland to the Forth, and beyond it a small plateau at Abronhill and then ground rising to Fannyside Muir. To the south-west the Luggie Water flowed out to the Clyde. Cumbernauld is on the watershed of central Scotland.

The 'St Enoch's Clock' came from the railway station of that name in Glasgow; it was unveiled by HM The Queen in 1977

'Radial' paving on a pedestrian way in Seafar

The town centre glimpsed from the pedestrian way approaching it from the south-west

Cumbernauld youths sit outside the 'Hollywood Bowl'

All the weather comes this way from everywhere, but especially from the west. In terms of climate it is a very exposed place, as was to be discovered when the famous 'Scottish Hurricane' struck it with wind speeds of up to 120 mph on a memorable January night in 1968.

The Plan

The plan provided for a tight urban place, suitable for a hilltop, with an absence of the satellite neighbourhoods and their centres which had been the hallmark of its predecessors. There was to be a single multi-purpose town centre with only small shops within the housing areas. The town centre was to stretch for half a mile along the hilltop itself, with a network of pedestrian routes leading both to it and through it. This was to be a town for pedestrians. The railway station to Glasgow was marooned on the southern extremity of the development. The 85% who were to come from that city were destined to find it not very easy to get back there! The road system, by contrast, was to lead to the centre and to the distributors circulating around the hill. The major junctions between these roads were to be grade separated. The Cumbernauld interchanges even today rival any to be found on the Scottish motorway system. In the late 1950s there was hardly a motorway in Britain, let alone in Scotland. This was mould-breaking stuff, indeed. The concrete bridges necessary for their implementation were the work of Ben Allen. They were innovative, sensitive, and with an almost Classical Doric clarity. They set standards in a field which was then only just opening up for structural engineers. Garages or parking places for 100% car ownership, pedestrian underpasses and bridges, high-density urban housing clustered on the slopes of the hill - Cumbernauld was surely going to set new trends in urban thought.

The flats in Kildrum, built by Jack Coia, whilst the Cumbernauld team was being assembled, have been refurbished and wrapped in new brickwork

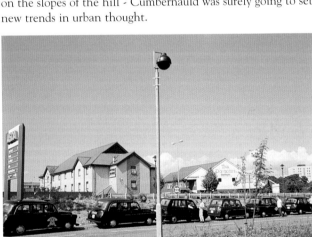

Taxi rank and 'cottage' style pubs and inns to the east of the town centre

McDonald's Restaurant on an 'island' site, difficult to reach by foot

There was to be some 'cottage' industry within the housing areas breaking accepted zonal planning assumptions, whilst major industry was to occupy the few areas of level ground on the periphery of the town.

From the beginning landscape was seen to be a key to containing so many people on such an improbable site. Peter Youngman was appointed consultant for this purpose. He proposed major structural tree planting, as a context and shelter for the other development. So successful has this been that today there are those who comment how fortunate the designers of Seafar were to have such lush natural woodland in which to build. But could it be achieved?

By 1961 the Scottish Office lifted the target population to 70,000 people. A revised plan in 1963 sought to accommodate these extra people by developing Abronhill and Condorrat. It was soon apparent, however, that even with eleven tower blocks on the hilltop, the target population could just not be achieved. The effort to do so was already distorting the design of the housing areas.

Out-of-town style traders on the town centre's St Mungo's Road

In 1973 the Secretary of State virtually doubled the designated area to the north of the A80 trunk road. A new lower-density community of 20,000 people was to be developed there in more scattered and broken terrain. Landscape was seen at the time as the likely unifying feature between this 'greater Cumbernauld' and the 'hilltop town'. According to the Extension Area Plan of 1974:

> The organisation of the built form and man-made landscape will in due course create the extension to Cumbernauld. Woven with the existing fabric with sensitivity and care they will emphasise the unity of the whole town.

The Sacred Heart RC Church, Kildrum

In practical terms the loose scattering of new settlements were to be linked by a snaking distributor road, tied back to the hilltop by interchanges at the west and east, and linked more directly by two footbridges, which eventually took the form of elegant single-pylon stayed structures designed by Tony Smith.

Although innovative high-density housing developments continued into the extended area at Westfield and Balloch by the early 1980s the changing public expenditure attitudes of Mrs Thatcher's first Conservative Administration meant that the rest of Cumbernauld was to be developed largely in lower-density housing by the private sector and other agencies.

The Plan Today

Cumbernauld and its plan was eventually, therefore, to be a Town of 'two halves': the 'first', the high-density urban cluster on its exposed hilltop with its associated tight satellites; the 'second', an extended 'suburb' across the valley, filling the open space which was once thought of as the essential lung for those living in a tight urban form.

Our Lady's RC High School and Ravenswood housing from Eastfield

As for the A80, it was advertised in the Extension Area Plan as being relocated to the Kelvin Valley, passing between the extended Cumbernauld and Kilsyth to the north. The intention was that there would be a new 'front window' view of the town: '... in the same way that the north side of the present town is seen from the A80 when approaching from the east or west, the northern parts of the extended town will form the first impressions of it from the new M80. ...In effect a new "front window" is being created.'

Almost a quarter of a century later the overwhelmed A80 still funnels 70,000 vehicles per day between each 'half' of Cumbernauld, dividing the hilltop town from its 'suburb' in the north. In February 1997 the Secretary of State announced that the location for the new motorway - the M80 - would be along

Abronhill Parish Church and Neighbourhood Centre

Community centre and shop created from the Kildrum Farm buildings

this existing route, rather than the northern route proposed in 1974. The leader of the new North Lanarkshire Council, Harry McGuigan, representing the views of Cumbernauld, has called for a public inquiry.

After forty years the Cumbernauld plan is still not resolved.

THE TOWN CENTRE

The visitor to Cumbernauld will be struck by the variety of styles and buildings which now occupy the exposed hilltop ridge; from the fragment of a multi-deck all-purpose centre at the west, to a 'prairie planning' superstore at the east, and all bounded on the south by a collection of one-off facilities which have the ambience of a kind of 'building bazaar'. What has happened? It is necessary to go back to the beginning.

The Burns Ale House, the Village - 'make-believe' history

A New Creation

The concept of the tight high-density hilltop town meant also that there would ideally be a similarly tight high-density 'urban' town centre, which would contain all the many and varied needs of a town of 50,000 people. The principal designer for this town centre was Geoff Copcutt. The solution was heavily informed by contemporary theories about 'mega-structures' as much as by the nature of the hilltop site itself. Its potential, as illustrated by sketches at the time, was immense. Its eventual failure was inherent within its concept, and the potential enormity of its cost.

Granite setts and dry-stone walling in Seafar

When building started in 1963 there is little doubt that it was heroic. Seen in the context of the times and the almost evangelical fervour which surrounded its conception and birth, it is just possible to understand why those concerned chose such a lonely furrow in comparison to contemporary town

Split-level housing in Liddel Road, Seafar, with new housing being built in the background - these are the larger Ravenswood split-level houses

centres. At the time there was something almost spiritual about the emerging *in-situ* mass concrete structure of the 'mega-structure' centre. The multi-deck design amounted to a correction of nature's own failure to quite complete the hilltop ridge. What was naturally rounded was partially excavated and in cross-section a 'pyramid' was created, which both linked the north and south of the hilltop, and also in a sense completed it. This leviathan was intended to stretch eventually along the whole ridge. It was to contain within its concrete skeleton all the elements of a multi-faceted traditional town centre: shops and housing, offices and restaurants, theatres and pubs, civic spaces and local government. All of this would soar over a dual-carriage Central Way taking traffic through the centre without being interrupted by it.

That this was also a draughty hilltop was recognised in that there was to be a 'wall' of 'windbreak' housing at the west end, shielding the semi-open streets in the sky from the western weather. The Corporation commissioned a comprehensive model of the whole centre as it would eventually be, and subjected it to wind-tunnel tests to refine the design of both the centre and its protecting wall of housing. The latter was never built.

Corner shop in white, Kenmore Road, Kildrum

The First Phase is Built

When it was completed in 1967 the first phase of the town centre was positively awesome, particularly when viewed from the west and the south. A many layered and faceted concrete structure, crowned with four banks of penthouses riding in the sky above it, and improbably supported on slender concrete fins.

On the first Hogmanay after its opening a television show was broadcast live from it to all of Scotland. The trombonist

Urban pedestrian way leading from Afton Road, Kildrum

The flats in Ivanhoe Road are repeated along the spine of Greenfaulds

Terraced housing and flats from Greenfaulds Road

George Chisholm was seen wandering along the echoing new malls, playing in the New Year. Hardly, however, had those echoes died away before some of the pride of achievement was beginning to fade. The concrete structure was pretty dour even in the sunshine, in the rain it was truly grim. Charles McKean has described it as: 'Grey, streaked and dominating...never gaining public affection'. The internal finishes were thin and meagre. The semi-open malls became wind tunnels themselves for the wind and the rain. Eventually a fortune had to be spent in glazed roofing and side enclosure, and thus also on new fire precautions. Even the external concrete was eventually painted to mask its dismal appearance.

The extended Burgh Chambers of Cumbernauld & Kilsyth District Council; the new North Lanarkshire Council has its HQ in Motherwell

A further but much smaller phase was added to it in similar style before it became apparent that the design of the Cumbernauld town centre was not the way in which shopping centres were developing elsewhere. Even the Golden Eagle Hotel, built to lock into the mega-structure had to be demolished because of structural failure, thereby pitching the town into almost two hotel-less decades. Only the imaginative and concrete Cumbernauld College remains of the many buildings which would have eventually locked into the mega-structure centre.

Lennox Road, trees and pedestrian way, Seafar

The Struggle for a Town Centre

The Corporation had immense difficulty in attracting major High Street retailers to come to the centre, or for that matter the funding for further developments, when it became clear that the public purse could not afford to bring this expensive dream to fruition and the population was slow in expanding. Eventually the then new Woolworth subsidiary, Woolco, was

The 'out-of-town' style superstore, surrounded by cars, east of the town centre

The Langlands/Seafar Interchange - landscape and simple concrete structures

attracted to the building of a superstore at the south-eastern end of phase one. With two levels of car parking beneath this store, desperate attempts were made in its design to bring it at least near to the existing shopping mall levels. It still, however, had to have its own individual entrance and parking directly accessed from Central Way. It was eventually taken over by Asda and demolished in the summer of 1996; Asda decamping to a traditional ground-level superstore in the east of the Central Area.

In the meantime, however, private money had been found to continue the development of the mixed-retail malls. This fourth phase of the centre, funded by a Pension Fund, was to be a ground-level mall on the north side of Central Way, and with both surface car parking and cars on its roof - the Cumbernauld Centre had been turned upside down.

Notwithstanding all of this, the centre today does present a fascinating place to be in; the entrance from Seafar and the relationship with the Parish Church of St Mungo's with its pyramid roof, demonstrates just what might have been.

Even within the only pieces of the original concept to be built, the changes of level, surprise vistas, nooks and crannies, squares and statues etc., all mean that internally this strange beast really does have many of the attributes of an older multi-purpose town centre - and all under one roof - or at least many related roofs.

In this sense, at least, the Cumbernauld town centre is an opportunity lost.

The Centre Today

In recent years the Development Corporation has struggled to be midwife to the completion of this unusual place. A 'stand alone' company was set up for this purpose - free to enter into developer partnerships. A scheme was developed to create

The future which 'might have been': the first phase of the town centre seen from the west; white paint now covers the drab concrete

St Mungo's Church of Scotland Parish Church on the north of the town centre

The Woolco store, a victory of sorts in the 1970s, is demolished

further ground-level shopping malls at the east and south of the existing malls, and the creation of a much-needed civic Town Square - all of this involving the closure of Central Way. This proposal stands stalled by the withdrawal of the chosen developer. The site of the Woolco store stands empty and abandoned. With the Development Corporation gone, the future is uncertain.

The fourth-phase shopping mall is at ground level with shoppers' cars sitting on the roof instead of beneath it

The Centre Revisited

Colin Cowan, Chief Executive from 1970 to 1986, observed: 'So it may be that the Centre was an innovation too far...but it has character!' Indeed it has.

The original concept, however, of a centre with so much under one roof was not wrong. Others have done it since - in part some of the other Scottish New Towns have done it - but not in what used to be called a 'rationalist brutalist structure'. In August 1995 the *Scotsman* carried a feature article by Miranda France, proclaiming the delights of the West Edmonton Mall in Alberta, Canada - 'the world's largest shopping centre'. In describing the sheer variety of services and activities present under one roof, she wrote: 'This mammoth mall provides all basic necessities, plus entertainment, lawyers and travel agents. You could conceivably spend your life in it.'

Forty years ago, Geoff Copcutt and Hugh Wilson could have echoed every word. That is all that they ever aspired to in their centre 'before its time'.

The first-phase shopping malls were originally lofty, dark and banner draped...

...they are now brighter - but somewhat diminished

TOWNSCAPE

There are many townscapes in Cumbernauld. The very nature of the topography which has already been described ensured that this would be the case. It is indeed a city set upon a hill,

The topography allows glimpses of other parts of the town from the 'hilltop'

The well-wooded north side of the 'hilltop' seen from the 'suburban' Eastfield

Trees and the town centre from the north

Grey roughcast seen through greenery in Abronhill

and for miles around it cannot be hidden. It is not, however, only the topography which has made a townscape in Cumbernauld. When Peter Youngman was appointed landscape consultant, he reported: 'The master plan must incorporate as much shelter planting as possible; the design must incorporate bold masses of trees on a scale large enough to contrast effectively with the close masses of buildings.'

Major tree planting in the early days of the town ensure that this is now the case; most strikingly seen on the north side of the hilltop with the high-rise blocks emerging from mature woodland, clusters of low-rise housing contained in a protecting canopy of green, and the town centre riding above on the ridge. This intention was carried into the extension area.

The 1974 plan stated: 'The major landscaping framework will be the network of open space into which the built environments will be integrated.'

The townscape of Cumbernauld is defined by a strong combination of its natural features with the landscape and building policies which have served to enhance them. This is particularly true within the original designated area. The overwhelming impression, however, of much of the earlier built environment was 'grey'! Wet-cast rendering and dour roughcast was used widely.

When the architectural journalist Ian Nairn visited the town in the late 1960s with a film crew he was to make much of this 'greyness', contrasting it with the brightly coloured wash walls of Scotland's east coast fishing villages. This use of grey building, however, especially within the housing areas, was seen in time to be the perfect backdrop to the enormous investment in public landscaping. Thus the eventual picture is one of light and shade, dappled reflection and colour in its season. Similarly the landscape backdrop is a frame for the many high-quality public buildings which grace the town, from fine churches to delightful schools.

The general townscape of Cumbernauld has both a unique character of its own, and has also created standards for others to follow, for it was in Cumbernauld that townscape was first regarded as a part of the design process in post-war Britain.

Cumbernauld Village

Cumbernauld also benefited from having within its designated area the existing villages of Condorrat and Cumbernauld. Although Condorrat was in a sense an industrial village, Cumbernauld had a street pattern of medieval origins, containing at the designation three fine churches, and some of the best remains of undeveloped 'lang riggs' in the country.

The treatment by the Corporation of the village has been sympathetic - its infill housing being in keeping and its 'lang riggs' conserved. The renaissance of the High Street, Baron Hill, Wynd and Smithyends uniquely balance commercial development with conservation. The village is not frozen history - it lives.

Town Art

Cumbernauld was the first of the New Towns in Scotland to appoint a Town Artist in the person of Brian Miller, but then lost that advantage by diverting most of his activity into creative promotional exhibition design. Notwithstanding, he produced a considerable number of innovative and colourful

The rear of properties in The Wynd, the Village

Cottages in Smithyends, the Village - built in the 1970s to restore the 'street'

The pedestrian approach from the south to the first phase of the town centre. The 'sculpture' was donated by the first Chairman, General Sir Gordon MacMillan, and unveiled by HRH The Princess Margaret

Michael Snowden's monumental *Mother and Child* in bronze in the shopping mall is hemmed in by teenagers

Only yards away from Snowden's sculpture is Bill Scott's rather more domestic *The Shopper*, also in bronze

Grey housing in Kilbowie Road, south Carbrain

Split-level houses, Seafar - granite setts and mature landscaping

Terrace housing with deeply recessed entrances, Kildrum

low-relief concrete murals, which are to be found around the town. He also specialised in gable end painted murals, most of which now seem to have been lost.

In comparison to the other towns, however, Cumbernauld lacks major sculpture in townscape situations. There are two splendid bronze pieces in the town centre shopping mall: Michael Snowden's monumental *Mother and Child* in bronze and, within a few yards of it, Bill Scott's rather more domestic *The Shopper,* also in bronze. There is also a local theme mural by Barbara Balmer .

HOUSING

Design Principles

From the beginning the design of housing in Cumbernauld was innovative. The earliest was designed principally by the multi-disciplinary teams set up by Hugh Wilson, with some undertaken by carefully selected Scottish consultant architects.

Jack Coia, later an RIBA Gold Medal-winner, had produced flats and houses in Kildrum virtually as the in-house teams were being assembled. The south-east English aesthetic of these blocks, however, served only to underline the contemporary 'traditional Scottish' interpretation of the housing design which came from the creativity of the Wilson team. This is particularly true of Kildrum. Whereas East Kilbride and Glenrothes had to that point used the known and accepted palette of Scottish public housing, the Cumbernauld designers set about creating both layout and house types from first principles.

Layout was heavily influenced by the pre-war United States community of Radburn, where the ideas of Clarence Perry on the separation of through transportation avenues from local roads and streets was first worked out. This was described by

Lewis Mumford as: '... the pedestrian paths and the vehicular roads form two independent systems.' Virtually all housing streets in Cumbernauld were to be culs-de-sac. The houses have their public access side, and their private side, in which the main habitable rooms overlook the private garden or patio. Garden fences are high to afford privacy. Considerable thought was given to topography and orientation with regard to both the sun shining in, and the resident's view out. Many houses overlook what was originally open countryside. It is hardly possible to describe all the housing within the town, but two examples from the earlier days will suffice to illustrate the principles and the problems.

Brown bricks come to the 'hilltop' - new flats in Hillcrest Avenue, north Carbrain

Innovative Design

At Seafar on the north side of the hilltop, the Corporation built split-level houses on relatively steep north-facing slopes, without resorting to massive underbuildings. With considerable skill a range of small two-storey houses was assembled within a landscape of silver birch trees, heather, and granite setts cast off from the streets of Glasgow. With ground-floor bedrooms and first-floor living rooms, the houses were, in effect, 'flats' set on the ground within a park. The whole has matured over almost forty years to be one of the finest housing environments in a New Town anywhere. The architect was Roy Hunter in collaboration with planner Bill Thomson. They have been much copied, even in Cumbernauld itself, but certainly never bettered.

Split-level houses, Seafar - new doors!

Problems of Density

On the gentler southern slopes of the hilltop in Carbrain, the high density of development and poor construction and

Lock-up garages in Ferguson Road, Seafar

The refurbished south Carbrain 'wall' of flats, and the pedestrian deck footbridge over Millcroft Road

materials, have led to pressures which have caused difficulty over three decades. The high-density 'wall' of houses and flats in South Carbrain, the latter with their elevated walkways were set to attract much criticism. Writing as long ago as 1977 in the *Architect's Journal*, Jim and Krystyna Johnson reported:

> …South Carbrain area where narrow-frontage three-storey houses and lumpy blocks of 6 & 7 storey walk-up flats, served by raised footpaths at first-floor level, had to be used to achieve densities in the region of 120 people per acre. This area with its unkempt and unloved raised walkways and extensive overlooking between houses is, as built, a sad retreat from the higher ideals of the first master plan and from the much better housing that came before, and after, in Cumbernauld.

Twenty years on and the 'lumpy' flats have already undergone major refurbishment, whilst the 'narrow houses' are in process of wholesale redevelopment. Sadly, even this effort is showing the signs of strain which come from high densities.

The concrete 'deck access' flats in Kenmore Road, Kildrum, were demolished …

…and replaced with altogether more fashionable brick housing

The contrast between this, and the sustained well-being of so much else of Cumbernauld's housing is a reminder that innovation isn't sufficient to ensure the future well-being of housing. It must also be well designed and credible to those who live within it, otherwise it will never be loved; and to grow old gracefully, housing must first be loved by those whose lives are largely spent within it.

Only the eleven concrete tower blocks on the hilltop can be said to have really broken Cumbernauld's own aspiration to be both creative and innovative. They came from the Government's intention to support a Scottish 'industrialised housing' industry but are redeemed by the sheer inventiveness of much of their garaging and hard and soft landscaping. The Corporation drew the line at allowing them to be let to families with children, and they became 'executive' homes.

The 1960s 'modern' Congregational Church with new flats beyond, Glenacre Road, north Carbrain

The Middle Years

Low-rise housing in Abronhill, Greenfaulds and Condorrat followed the established pattern of excellence, perhaps eventually losing something of the first love and excitement. In moving into the extended designated area, however, the designers appeared to recover their nerve and produced a renewed commitment to innovative design.

This is demonstrated in Westfield with its densely landscaped communal courtyards which offer a magnificent public side to the grouped two-storey terraces, almost obscuring them with natural growing things. In Balloch the designers produced a winding village street, centred upon a community shop, and with the parking courts accessed through arched vennels.

Blind-side 'patio' houses in Lochlea Road, Kildrum

Terraced houses in Abronhill

Garages and flats in Medlar Road, Abronhill

Housing Court off Woodhead Road, Westfield

There had been a decade-long gap in the recognition of Cumbernauld housing by the Saltire Society. Westfield and Balloch were 'commended' in 1979 and 1981 respectively. Both have worn the succeeding years gracefully, despite their continuing high-density form.

Housing in the 'Suburb'

For the rest, the extended designated area of Cumbernauld has largely provided a home for speculative private housing developers. What was to have been a 25% share of the housing cake in the 1974 plan became, under the Conservative Government of the 1980s, the 'norm' for development. Even the Mainhead Woodland, sitting at 500 feet above sea-level and looking out to the north over the Kelvin Valley, has been filled with houses in the modern developer styles - from 'mock Georgian' to 'improbable Tudor'. Each of the 'estates' of private houses is accessed through stylised 'gateways' of gateless gateposts, each to denote in the future a 20mph zone. Even the Balloch 'village street' now has its formal gateposts.

Executive housing built in the Mainhead Woodland at Queen's Drive, Westerwood

There is, however, the beginnings of another 'village' street at Craigmarlock, 400 feet up, with a village square and urban scale protecting blocks of flats. Ironically its first design consultant was Gillespies, founded thirty years ago by William Gillespie, the first Principal Landscape Architect in the town, and who, with Peter Youngman, was responsible for so much of the landscaping on the hilltop.

It was the anticipated exposure, however, of the developable land in the extension area which led the 1974 Report to state:

> The degree of weather exposure likely to be experienced in the Town Extension makes it essential that large-scale landscaping proposals provide some protection from prevailing winds and driving rain, and help to create sheltered areas for housing, open space and other uses, wherever possible.

Detached house at King's Drive, Westerwood, looks out over the Kelvin Valley

'Cottage' at Weavers Brae, Craigmarloch

It is not apparent that this has yet happened to the extent intended.

INDUSTRY

Much of Cumbernauld's early factory building was in itself innovative. Notched north light roofs and plain white walls made Blairlinn in its day a state-of-the-art place to locate for industrialists. The 'cottage' industry within residential areas is best seen in Seafar at the 'flatted factory'. Similarly Cumbernauld pioneered the 'advance' factory, designed and built to attract potential industry; also 'nest' factories - in effect desirable workshops. Sadly, much of this early industrial effort is now largely run-down and in need of major refurbishment if it is to continue to serve the town in the future.

Early Corporation-built factories at Blairlinn

'Standard' factory at Lenziemill

The Broadwood Business Park

Small and colourful 'nest' factories in Westfield

Like other New Towns in Scotland Cumbernauld has itself purpose-built facilities for incoming industrialists, although the town's most prominent factory, Burrough's at Wardpark, was under construction at the time of the designation. Like the other Scottish New Towns which had Burrough's on board, Cumbernauld was to suffer the pain of its departure. The factory is now occupied by OKI, which have also been social benefactors in the town, materially contributing to the new football stadium.

The major new industrial parks at the western entrance to the town, created as a part of the extended designated area, have become a focus for high-quality high-tech factories. Also at Broadwood, the beginnings of a modern Business Park, the worth of which cannot yet be judged; but the potential, sitting by a new artificial loch, is considerable.

SUMMARY

Cumbernauld is a little like the proverbial curate's egg - good in parts. In fact, it is very good in parts. Its innovative potential was considerable, and much of its planning, layout, housing and landscaping, has been of a high order. It has set standards to which others have aspired. Its influence worldwide has been immense.

Even in the low-density 'other half' in the extended designated area, it is possible to see an emerging and eventually attractive 'suburb'.

There are clouds, however, over Cumbernauld. How will the town centre ever become the modern and attractive destination which the town now so clearly needs? Is it too late? Can the higher-density housing in Carbrain ever be given the confidence to become a more self-sustaining environment? Will the distant North Lanarkshire Council in Motherwell be able to cope with the resource implications of the large public landscape estate? Are standards already slipping?

To fulfil itself and to best serve its people, Cumbernauld will need care, and it will need investment. It is far from complete.

Graffiti on the forbidding underpass leading from the Park to the Village

A new 'standard' industrial unit in Westfield

Chapter Five

LIVINGSTON — *The Second-Best Place to Live in Britain?*

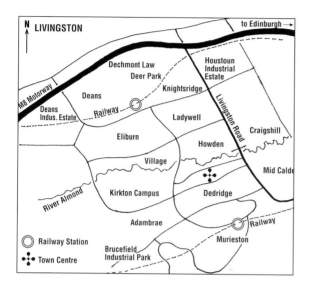

LIVINGSTON

to Edinburgh →

Dechmont Law
Deer Park

Houstoun
Industrial
Estate

Knightsridge

M8 Motorway

Deans

Deans
Indus. Estate

Railway

Ladywell

Livingston Road

Craigshill

Eliburn

Howden

Village

Mid Calde

River Almond

Kirkton Campus

Dedridge

Adambrae

Railway

Railway Station

Town Centre

Brucefield
Industrial Park

Murieston

- *Location:* West Lothian

- *Designated:* 1962

- *Area:* 6692 acres

- *Population:* 45,000

INTRODUCTION

Livingston lies in West Lothian, a county known in the past for being one of Scotland's cradles of industrial development. Coal was mined here, shale oil extracted and early manufacturing industry developed. A claim that a New Town built here could be the 'Second-Best Place to Live in Britain' rather seems to lack credibility.

The claim, however, was made not by the town's Development Corporation, but by geographers from the 'Quality of Life Group' in Strathclyde University. In a report published in January 1997 Dr Robert Rogerson and his team rated Livingston second in a ranking of 189 small cities and towns in the United Kingdom.

Sitting in the gentle valley of the river Almond, Livingston is the antithesis of the older industrial communities elsewhere in the Scottish central lowlands.

A striking, modern and well-mannered town, its 'town centre in the valley' is the opposite of Cumbernauld's 'town centre on the hill'. Instead, Livingston is a town held in the bowl of a pastoral valley, with the town centre lying on the banks of the river itself.

This parkland town prides itself on being at the heart of Scotland's 'Silicon Glen', and has been in the forefront of bringing high-tech inward investment into the central belt.

Almondvale Park with the Almond Valley Bridge in the background; countryside follows river Almond through the heart of the town

Abstract **in stainless steel by Denis Barns is a long-standing symbol of Livingston; it is located at the Dedridge Burn Greenway to the east of the Almondvale Centre**

New speculative office symbolises Livingston's high-tech image, Almondvale Way, Almondvale

Livingston Football Stadium, Almondvale

Grade separation as a bus approaches the Almondvale Centre

Shadowed and toned houses in Gowanbank, Ladywell

The access to Ladywell from Howden East, with Cousland Road passing beneath the bridge

Livingston is far from being a secret town - and will be remembered by a generation of Londoners who might never even have been to Scotland, but who have subliminally absorbed the haunting message of the town's poster adverts on the London Underground escalators - *Make it in Livingston*. Around 45,000 people have done just that.

THE LOCATION

Livingston lies in the valley of the river Almond some 15 miles west of Edinburgh; Glasgow is 30 miles to the west. Both cities are easily reached by the M8 which passes through the northern part of the designated area. The southern of the two railway lines between these two cities also passes through the town, with the Livingston South railway station providing access to its services. There is a railway line from Bathgate to Edinburgh which passes through the northern part of the town and the Livingston North railway station is located on it. Edinburgh Airport is only 10 miles away, and the older industrial town of Bathgate is almost contiguous to the north-west.

THE STORY

Changing Times

The problems experienced by the City of Glasgow with regard to its 'overspill' population did not cease with the designation of Cumbernauld in 1955, despite the many difficulties and debates which attended the birth of Britain's only New Town of the 1950s. By contrast to these difficulties the progress towards the designation of Livingston as a New Town was considerably easier. In part this was because of changing

Pedestrian bridge over the river Almond links the Almondvale Centre to Almondvale Park

Government attitudes towards development, and a realisation that the 'tiered regional approach', involving frequent references to London, was simply not able to respond adequately to the developing social, economic and physical planning issues inherent in a rapidly changing society.

New Ways to do Things

In 1960 the Secretary of State commissioned a study into these issues - particularly the Scottish Economy - under the chairmanship of J.N. Toothill of Ferranti Ltd. The publication of this report in 1961 was a major contribution to the developing debate about regional development in Scotland as a springboard for economic growth. The debate, in a sense, was a precursor of the discussion which eventually led to the establishing of the Regional Councils in 1975.

The great 'plans' of the immediate post-war period had served to highlight their limitations with regard to their implementation.

The first thing to happen after Toothill was the setting up of the National Economic Development Council to promote regional growth policy, and then the Scottish Development Department as an arm of the Scottish Office in promoting and executing both regional planning and its infrastructure.

Amidst this seed change in attitudes the Draft Designation Order for Livingston was published on 15 January 1962. Livingston was to be a town which enjoyed a consensus of purpose. The target population of 70,000 people was not seen as a 'colony' of the city in the countryside - Glasgow was after all rather a long way away - but as the hub of a Regional Plan. This was the Lothians Regional Plan

Controlled surface pedestrian crossing at Howden South

Carefully crafted pedestrian way by the Dedridge Burn

Pedestrian underpass to Alderstone Business Park

published in 1964 and covering a population of some quarter of a million people. Also by the end of 1963 the Scottish Development Department had produced a White Paper, 'Central Scotland: A Programme for Development and Growth'. Livingston was to be a principal growth area within it.

Livingston is Designated

The town was formally designated on 7 April 1962. The Designation Order itself made it quite clear that Livingston was not simply to be there to provide homes for Glaswegians with a yen to travel:

> ...a new town would offer the possibility not merely of helping solve Glasgow's housing problem but also of using overspill constructively to create a new focus of industrial activity in the central belt of Scotland...revitalising with modern industries an area hitherto over-dependent on coal and shale.

There seems here also to be an acknowledgement that Glasgow's industries were not 'moving' to new towns, or indeed to anywhere else. They were simply 'dying'. There needed to be new catalysts for economic activity and employment, and Livingston was to be one of them - not just a place for those spilt over from the crowded city in the west, but a new beginning for West Lothian as well.

Brown brick housing and bare landscape in Ladywell

The site was some 6692 acres, making it half as big again as Cumbernauld, which had also just had its target population raised to 70,000.

The Development Corporation

There was a high-profile launch of the town, and the Board held its first meeting immediately following. The Chairman

Pedestrian way between Rushbank and Ryebank, Ladywell

A pedestrian pend leads to a residential square in Manitoba Avenue, Howden

was Sir David Lowe, an agriculturist. William Taylor, lawyer and Convener of Glasgow Corporation Planning Committee, was Vice-Chairman, becoming Chairman after Sir David. William Taylor was at the time a noted activist and popular speaker on the planning issues of the day. Midlothian and West Lothian County Councils were represented, as also was the Scottish business community - including the General Manager of Rolls-Royce, themselves located in East Kilbride. The first General Manager when appointed was Brigadier Arthur Purches who came from the similar post in Glenrothes. The first Chief Architect and Planning Officer was Peter Daniel, who uniquely combined professional qualifications in town planning, architecture and landscape architecture. He had experience of housing design in Peterlee New Town in County Durham.

Offices for Walker Homes in Royston Road, Deans Industrial Estate

THE PLAN

The Lothian Regional Survey and Plan of 1964 and the White Paper of 1963 made Livingston the first Scottish New Town to be placed within a concurrent regional planning context. Important for the town in the former study was that the Livingston town centre should be a 'sub-regional centre for shopping, commerce, entertainment and service facilities'.

The plan for the town was made by the Peter Daniel team and, as already indicated, placed this sub-regional centre in the heart of the valley on the southern banks of the river Almond. The plan brings a principal road - the A899 / Livingston road - in from the M8 at Junction 3, to pass in a north to south direction at the eastern end of the designated area, and linking in the south with the A71 from Edinburgh to the west. This grade-separated dual carriageway itself gives access to the town

Livingston Road A899 runs south from the M8, making a main access 'spine' to the town

The refurbished Craigshill Neighbourhood Centre

Pedestrian way in Dedridge - a 'Greenway' running into the town

Diagnostic Sonar, Simpson Parkway, Kirkton Campus

roads, which in turn access the distributor roads. Virtually all of these latter junctions are at grade. The town roads define the different 'areas' of the town.

The town centre was designed not simply to be 'sub-regional', but also to be a 'local' centre for the housing communities nearest to it within the valley. Only Craigshill, to the east of Livingston Road, and Deans - out of the valley and north of the Edinburgh to Bathgate railway line - were to have neighbourhood centres as such, the latter being located with the eventual Livingston North railway station. Like its predecessor New Towns in Scotland, Livingston's town centre was not to have a rail link. This was again a bus, car and taxi town.

A major aspect of the plan and its subsequent development has been the use of 'Greenways': linear pedestrian links, which bring the countryside into the heart of the town, and also linking the major areas of open space and parkland. The immediate valley of the Almond was to be developed as a linear green 'lung' running through the heart of the town.

The principal industrial areas were located on the east and west of the designated area, with an effective 'front window' estate - Deans, straddling the M8. Livingston was generally developed from east to west, which means that it is in the west that the main areas still awaiting development are to be found.

THE TOWN CENTRE

The whole central area of Livingston has been given a brand name, the Almondvale Centre, and this is vigorously promoted within the town, even to zone signs of colourful design as the centre is approached. The first phase of the shopping centre itself was opened in 1977. Over the years before and after,

The Almondvale 'brand name' greets the visitor on the approaches to the town centre

much else was built in the way of other town centre destinations and facilities, but it was to be almost 20 years, 1996, before the second phase of the shopping centre was opened. Livingston learned the same lesson as the other Scottish New Towns - that you cannot have a successful shopping centre until you first have a population.

The south-eastern entrance to the Almondvale Centre, past the Bank of Scotland

The First Phase of Shops

That first phase opened in 1977 was typical of its day; inward-looking, covered, it presented a largely blank exterior to the outside world. It was, however, in many senses ingenious, making good use of the gently sloping ground to accommodate service roads, and in being linked to a well-designed multi-storey car park. Pedestrian access from the east tended to be a little troglodyte, but the adjacent landscaping and road structures were of an urban scale.

The Second Phase of the Centre

This latest developer-procured slice of shopping centre reflects all the changes in practice and expectations which have taken place since the 1970s. It is no longer acceptable that shopping centres should be solely inward-looking, they must now also be attractive and welcoming places from the outside as well - and the Almondvale Centre most certainly is.

One of the two squares in the first phase of the Almondvale Centre

It is a turreted affair, set within large areas of open-air surface car parking. It is, in this sense at least, more 'out of town' shopping than 'in town'. Banded red and toned brick, pitch roofed, girt with pagoda-like flanking entrance towers, and crowned with a magnificent town clock, the Almondvale Centre now presents a strikingly attractive destination. Its

The Safeway superstore at the Almondvale Centre - integrated 'out-of-town' shopping

The northern entrance towers to the Almondvale Centre

The western entrance towers and town clock, Almondvale Centre - seen across the surface car park

The Almondvale Boulevard looking east

Colonnade and arches in Livingston Square, lying between the Almondvale Centre and Almondvale Park

The Hilton Hotel in Almond View marks the eastern edge

principal entrances are obvious and inviting. There is a separately entranced Safeway superstore built in similar style as the current west end 'anchor'.

The discipline of this building design is carried through to the exterior spaces, both for pedestrians and cars. There is high-quality paving in paviors and slabs reflecting the building itself, there are red bobble cluster lamp standards and fetching red bollards everywhere.

The Almondvale Boulevard & Livingston Square

Running along the north side of this centre is the Almondvale Boulevard: a formal tree-lined, traffic-controlled avenue, which makes extensive use of different surface textures and colours.

To the north of this again, and opposite one of the principal entrances to the centre, is the new Livingston Square, designed by Gillespies - flesh-yellow stone, colonnaded and metal arched. It is formal in concept and graced with an effervescent bronze sculpture by Charles Anderson; this is an improbable expression of energetic young people defying gravity to reach for the sky. Whether or not it is a metaphor for Livingston is perhaps less important than its role as a community focus within the centre. It is appropriately named *The Community*. It presides over formal planting and vivid flowers in season. This square is linked to the delightful Almondvale Park by a pedestrian suspension bridge over the river Almond.

At its eastern end the Boulevard gives access to the low-rise Hilton International Hotel, and at its west end to the Bubbles Leisure Centre - pink and grey striped with a blue roof - the latter enhanced by a corner sculpture in yellow sandstone, *Symbioses*, by Madeline Weiner. Opposite Safeway is a long two-storey yellow brick building with overhanging eaves and containing the Clydesdale Bank and the local Law Courts.

Symbioses by Madeline Weiner graces the Bubbles Leisure Centre on Almondvale Boulevard

The *Windvane Family* by Philip Johnson on the Boulevard Roundabout marks the western edge of the Almondvale Centre

The Boulevard Roundabout

The Boulevard ends in the west at the Boulevard Roundabout with its dramatic *Windvane Family* by Philip Johnson. This comprises four giant humanoid 'space' figures, each topped with kinetic drooping wind vanes. This western end of the Almondvale Centre is still fairly empty, more 'thistles' than 'things' - the *Windvane Family* stamp their authority upon this petering out of the Almondvale Centre. They also represent a striking feature of an enlightened Development Corporation policy to bring contemporary urban sculpture to strategic locations within the town.

The Centre Periphery

The rest of the periphery of the Almondvale Centre sports its carpet stores and DIY palaces, as well as the free-standing McDonalds Restaurant - there is one inside as well.

Off Almondvale South is the gloomy, shed-like 'soon to be replaced' bus station, the anonymous brown brick police station, the white horizontal-striped, multi-storey Pentland House (to match Sidlaw House on the north) and a rather neatly tiered Bank of Scotland.

Like Glenrothes, Livingston is fortunate in having the many jobs which go with the location of the new West Lothian Council within the town. The new council appears determined to support Livingston's role as the new principal town of West Lothian.

The McDonald's Restaurant on Almondvale West

The Divisional Police Office on Almondvale South

THE MALLS

The visitor to the Almondvale Centre experiences two very distinct phases.

The first phase is characterised by low but well-lit shopping malls linking two top-lit and much higher squares, which were

The main entrance hall and food court, Almondvale Centre - with Moorish overtones

The new second-phase mall - wide, bright and welcoming

Howden House and its mature south-facing parkland are in the heart of the town

the focus of the earlier centre. These spaces are 'destinations', with 'sit-out' eating places, colourful stalls, lottery kiosks and the rest. At two and half times the height of the adjacent malls there is a real sense of scale and space, which is multiplied by the clever use of mirror glass on the wall surfaces.

Then, there is the second phase, opened in 1996. The link between the two is dramatic: from the enclosed low mall, to a lofty, white, glazed vault. A bright, reflective floor, palm trees in pots and the inevitable banners hanging down like regimental colours hanging in the nave of a Gothic cathedral. Along the line of the ridge of this glazed vault, white hanging lanterns form part of the night-time illumination. The glory of this centre, however, is the northern entrance area and food hall. With arched side aisles and a number of large palm trees, it has a modest 'Moorish' atmosphere. People are clearly happy to linger within it. This is the principal face of this attractive centre. This is where most visitors to the Centre arrive. And everywhere, above you, below you, alongside you, the Almondvale Centre 'brand' signs and logos to press home the point that this is Livingston, and they want you to know it!

THE TOWNSCAPE

Livingston's townscape is largely made by its topography, gently blended with the built environment and landscape planting which is evidence of 35 years of creativity on the part of its builders. Most, although not all, of the town is located within the shallow valley of the Almond, with its mature tree planting, and parkland surrounding Howden House.

The Development Corporation planted large numbers of trees, which both complement the existing, and are a delight in their own right. To this they added their unique 'Greenways',

Almondvale seen from Howden Park

forming a network of fingers of countryside tracing their way through the town, and providing also a major pedestrian system. Within this tracery of green, the natural flora and fauna of the West Lothian countryside has been brought to this urban place. There are song birds in their season, herons the year round, roe deer like wraiths haunting the shaded woodland.

Geese on the pond on the Dedridge Burn, within sight of the town centre

The centre of this system is the Almond Vale itself, which forms a green delight running through the heart of the town and linking the countryside to the east and to the west. The highlight of this river park is the sweep of the Livingston Road Bridge, simple, dignified, seeming to glide across the sky above the valley floor. Beneath it the landscape and water features are rich and diverse.

Road bridge carrying Alderstone Road over the River Almond

Most of the housing and principal buildings of Livingston appear as springing from the green mantle of trees which contains them. Like all the New Towns, Livingston has many buildings which are excellent in their own right, although some of the primary schools have a dreary ambience. On the other hand, the St Margaret's Academy is a delight, riding above the carpet of trees to the north of the Almond.

The St John's District Hospital is a massive place. However bland its architecture, it is a statement of conviction about the nature of Livingston. It provides services to the whole region, which is what Livingston is increasingly about. As a piece of townscape it dominates the whole northern slope of the Almond Vale.

St Margaret's Academy, Howden South, seen from the south across the river Almond

The neighbourhood centre at Carmondean in Deans gives a first appearance of a supermarket and bleak car park. It also embraces, however, competent buildings for a health centre, library, public house and church. Livingston has many

St Peter's RC Church, Carmondean Centre

St John's District Hospital, Howden

Industrial 'classical' standard units on the southern edge of the Kirkton Campus

churches, some more ambitious as architecture than others. It is the only Scottish New Town to have achieved a full-blown Ecumenical Project amongst the mainstream churches. This has given the town at least one ecumenical building of interest at the Lanthorn Centre in Dedridge - the architecture might be anonymous, the intention however is revolutionary.

The earliest of the Industrial Estates, Houstoun, is fairly solidly built up, but with the old Cameron Ironworks providing a skyline punctuation alongside the M8. This landmark can be seen almost from the Forth Road Bridge, and is now as much a feature of this landscape as the remaining shale bings. By contrast, the Kirkton Campus in the west of the town is about shiny, high-tech factories nestling within a deep green forest and expansive parkland.

The 'other' townscape of Livingston is the ribbon of industrial development which is visible from the M8. This has long been a 'taste of other things'. A way of saying, 'You really should come in and have a look!' Some of it is that good, some not. In its last year, however, the Development Corporation has marked Junction 3 on the motorway with a large stone and copper archway. Under the name of *Norgate*, a dramatic icon by David Wilson is reminiscent of the whalebone arches which have graced the entrances of many Scottish country estates. It defines the principal entry to the town.

There is also a Beefeater Hotel and Restaurant in the same location, in that comfortable contemporary British 'traditional' style which has come to mark out successful business communities. Beyond is Denchmont Law which has the effect of providing a shield from the motorway for the high-value private housing developments of Deer Park.

***Norgate*, by David Wilson, marks the entrance to Livingston from the M8**

'Exclusive' private housing, Golf Course Road, Deer Park

Livingston Village

The former shale-oil village of Livingston Station was translated into Deans, although most of the essential elements of its fabric remain within the larger community. The historic village of Livingston, however, clustered around its church, has been allowed to assume the atmosphere of a fragment of 'somewhere else' within the expanding urban town. Its rehabilitation has been sparing and careful.

HOUSING

Livingston, like others, fell prey at its beginning to the blandishments of the 'industrialised' housing industry and the bullying of Government, with the result that one of its early employers was a factory making 'Laing 12M Jesperson' homes. The system was Scandinavian, and the houses and flats it produced were built at Craigshill in concrete panel and infill timber. They were once one of the wonders of 'modern' Scotland, with councillors and architects from all over the country being wined and dined to assist their appreciation of them. That they were also deeply unsatisfactory, unpopular, damp and downright ugly is now a matter of record and history. What the Development Corporation has done with their refurbishment and replacement is contemporary and remarkable.

A judicious mixture of demolition, reconstruction and replacement has produced an altogether delightful and colourful environment. It is an exemplar to others as to how to tackle such difficult situations.

The 1960s and early 1970s were for Livingston a time of fairly standard housing, now redeemed by the high quality of its landscaping. As the 1970s wore on, however, and Livingston made extensive use of 'common' house types from the palette of the time, so did their inventive use of creative layout and carefully targeted colour. The result is a considerable estate of high quality and very liveable housing areas; even though Knightsridge East has had to be revisited and 'thinned' out to reduce the densities. There are walk-up square blocks of flats in Livingston, but no high-rise. This is a low-rise town.

The Jesperson 'piano' blocks, Craigshill - enjoying their last springtime in 1994...

...and as imaginatively redesigned and constructed in 1996

Some of the blocks were demolished and created space for newer and more traditional housing

Earth reds enhance the houses in Sutherland Way, Knightsridge

'Thinned out' housing in Logan Way, Knightsridge

Careful private housing, Kirk Lane, Livingston Village

The NEL Factory in Carnegie Road, Deans Industrial Estate - a 'front of shelf' employer north of the M8

Typical well-designed small factory, Caputhall Road, Deans Industrial Estate

'Standard' industrial units in Dunlop Square, Deans Industrial Estate

Mitsubishi Electric in a high-grade plant, Houstoun Industrial Estate

The private housing, as in the other New Towns, is different in character, colour and materials, from the earlier housing. It reflects the changing aspirations of our times. There is a wide range of opportunity and design, demonstrating a vigorous local housing market, which is reflected also in Housing Association developments. This has clearly made Livingston a destination for those seeking a good place to both live and work.

INDUSTRY

There has already been reference made to the industrial estates of Houstoun and Kirkton. The concept of the latter apparently arose from a visit to the site by the then Chief Architect, Bill Brown, and his Estate Officer colleague.

The rest is about the sheer high quality of architectural achievement, both by the Development Corporation's own architects, and by consultants working for many, many developers. There is colour, there is fine detail, there is quality of materials, there is rich and detailed landscape, and overall a sense that these must largely be very satisfactory places in which to work.

In the development of places for both factories and offices, Livingston has demonstrated that quality attracts quality. That whatever might be said by individual industrialists in isolation, it is quite possible to create the kind of high-quality industrial and commercial environment to which they will be anxious to gain entry. This is what Livingston has achieved.

Livingston has amply fulfilled the objective of being a catalyst in the regeneration of the economy of West Lothian. During the time of the development of Livingston, the nearby

British Leyland Truck & Van Plant at Bathgate has been, and has gone. Today, however, there is Motorola at Bathgate - they wanted to be in Livingston, but a suitable site could not be found. Well, if you can't 'Make it in Livingston', it appears that the next best thing is to 'Make it nearby'! This has to be good news for the whole West Lothian area, and what catalysts of excellence should be all about.

A factory in the countryside, Kirkton Campus, seen from Simpson Parkway

SUMMARY

Livingston Development Corporation has left its charge at a time when it can take satisfaction from much that has been achieved. In the western part of the town, however, much has still to be achieved. The eventual outcome will be a considerable test of the plans and arrangements already made, and for the new West Lothian Council.

In other ways, also, the responsibilities now falling upon others will be considerable.

Mirror glass, the Canon factory, Fleming Road, Kirkton Campus

Amongst much excellence, Livingston has housing areas which are showing the physical stress of relatively high-density living. The Loan, an excellent pedestrian route down through Ladywell and Howden, is a focus for graffiti. This is blighting the many well-designed community facilities grouped along its length. Aware of the graffiti problem in parts of the town the Development Corporation has even held 'summer schools' for graffiti artists - the success of which is evidenced by the artistic value of some of the art form. Similarly there are signs of distress in the landscaping in parts of these two areas, highlighting the issue of future maintenance.

Yet another attractive small unit in Kirkton Campus

Livingston, however, has done its best to focus on excellence. This is to be seen in the Almondvale Centre as well as in the later industrial and commercial developments. The Development Corporation has not been content to die with a whimper, but has chosen to mark its passing with success - particularly its commitment in its closing years to dramatic urban sculpture and town art. It has given a unique urban feature to their town. They did 'make it in Livingston'. It is hoped that many others will follow its example.

Graffiti under the Alderstone Road Bridge over the river Almond - the Development Corporation even ran 'summer schools' for graffiti artists

***The Paraffin Harvester* by David Moore with West Lothian House (formerly Sidlaw House) in the background**

Chapter Six

IRVINE – *I do like to be beside the seaside!*

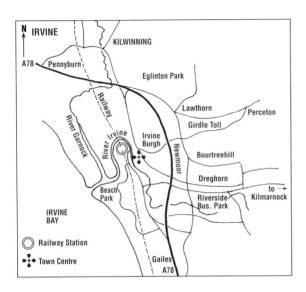

The historic Harbour made Irvine an important trading centre

- *Location :* North Ayrshire

- *Designated :* 1966

- *Area :* 12,409 acres

- *Population :* 55,5000

INTRODUCTION

Irvine was an important port on the Ayrshire coast long before governments of the United Kingdom began to think about the planting of New Towns.

Granted a Royal Charter from the King of Scotland in 1372 it was to be the chief port for Glasgow until the deepening of the Clyde in the eighteenth century. It was also the administrative centre for North Ayrshire.

The Royal Burgh of Irvine is an ancient place in its own right. It was the last of the five New Towns in Scotland to be designated under the post-war New Towns Acts. It is the only New Town in Britain on a coastal site, and the only one in Scotland to be centred on a substantial existing population. Its two existing burghs of Irvine and Kilwinning, and other villages, had a population of 34,500 people at the time of the designation. Today it is a vigorous and attractive place in which the old and the new have been carefully and imaginatively integrated. It has been widely recognised in the receipt of Awards for its design excellence.

LOCATION

Irvine is located 25 miles to the south of Glasgow and 6 miles west of Kilmarnock. East Kilbride is 20 miles away to the north-east.

Terrace housing, Glenapp Place, Pennyburn

The town is situated on the river Irvine which flows to Irvine Bay at the Harbour.

The A78 coastal route passes through the town. It is joined in Irvine by the A71 from Edinburgh. The main Glasgow to Stranraer railway lies to the west of the town centre.

The river Irvine from the north - the Rivergate Centre and the spire of the Trinity Centre in the east

THE STORY

In 1963 the Scottish Office published a White Paper, 'Central Scotland: A Programme for Development and Growth'. It had been prepared by the new Scottish Development Department. This policy document was about identifying areas which would be appropriate for growth and therefore suitable cases for financial aid from the Government. This was seen as an alternative to simply offering support to areas of decline.

Livingston, as we have already seen, was identified as a 'growth point' and became a New Town. That Irvine also became a 'growth point' had much to do with the considerable efforts which it had already made upon its own behalf.

The A78 trunk road runs north/south through Irvine New Town

Irvine Town Council

In many senses the vigour of the local Ayrshire community has much in common with the community in Fife, perhaps reflecting their common experience of a failing coal-mining industry.

Thus in 1959 Irvine Town Council had purchased the site of the former Irvine Royal Ordnance Factory, some 180 acres of valuable development land to the west of the town centre. In the early 1960s the councillors of Irvine were much in the Scottish news media on account of their vigorous and successful programme of industrial expansion, which brought

The western entrance to the Rivergate Shopping Centre - in the 'conservatory' style

The Tourist Information Office, New Street, with Cunninghame House in the background

'Traditional' infill housing at the junction of Burns Street and Castle Street, Irvine Burgh

Irvine Town House, High Street, Irvine Burgh

A 'very' public toilet, Riverside Walk

over sixty new companies to the Burgh. Like Glenrothes, Irvine was eventually to prosper as a New Town not only as a result of Government diktat, but through the efforts of its local politicians - men such as Provost Alex Rubie, Councillor Wilson Muir and, by no means least, the then Town Clerk, Bert White.

That Irvine was designated as a New Town perhaps also had much to do with the election in October 1964 of a new Labour Government under Harold Wilson. Building upon the work already done under the previous administration, the new Secretary of State for Scotland, William Ross - himself an Ayrshire man - had by January 1965 commissioned Wilson & Wolmersley, Consultant Planners and Architects, to prepare a report and plan for a possible New Town 'around and including Irvine and Kilwinning'.

A New Town in Irvine

Hugh Wilson had only recently left his position as Chief Architect and Planner in Cumbernauld for a life in private consultancy. Under the new Government he became an adviser to the Minister for Housing and Local Government, Richard Crossman, and was to conduct him on a visit to Cumbernauld in February 1965 whilst his team was working on the Irvine plan. His partner, Lewis Wolmersley had been the City Architect of Sheffield and gained considerable reputation for his design of the famous 'streets in the air' flats at Parkhill, Sheffield.

The consultants submitted their interim plan within the four months in May 1965. The Secretary of State, after appropriate consultation, published the Draft Designation

Order in February 1966. The New Town was to cover an area of 12,400 acres including the burghs of Irvine and Kilwinning and the village of Dreghorn. There was a Public Inquiry in July 1966 and the Designation Order was confirmed on 9 November 1966.

The target population was to be 116,000 people, later reduced in 1981 to 95,000. In May 1967, only two years after the submission of their original interim plan, the finalised Wilson & Wolmersley proposals were published under the title, 'The Irvine New Town Planning Proposals'.

Footpath between Gottries Place and Harbour Street - flanked by sweeping white walls

The Development Corporation

The Development Corporation Board held its first meeting in June 1967. The Chairman was A.W.Hardie. The first Managing Director was Denis Kirby who began in early 1968, having worked in the Colonial Service and in the Foreign Office. He came to Irvine, however, from a high-profile and successful four-year period as the General Manager of East Kilbride, then reaching its peak of success. He was to stay with Irvine for the first critical years of its existence, leaving in 1972 to take up the post of Industrial Director for Scotland with the Department of Trade & Industry. He was succeeded by Jim Marquis who had been the Finance Officer.

The first Chief Architect and Planner was David Gosling, a young man with wide qualifications in architecture, civic planning and town planning, gained in Britain and the USA. He was, like Hugh Wilson before him, to gather around him a team of young and enthusiastic professionals.

The YMCA Building: Caley House, Howgate, Kilwinning

Perceton House - home to the Development Corporation for most of its life

Problems

The early years of the New Town were marked by considerable difficulty, principally generated by the extent of old mine

Moorfoot Place, Bourtreehill, through a pedestrian pend - sett walls and shady trees

Private housing, Burnbrae Drive, Perceton - Baronial brick

Lawthorn Church of Scotland, Inkwood Court, Lawthorn

St John Ogilvy RC Church, Bourtreehill Village Centre

workings, and also problems with land ownership. As a consequence, a revised interim outline plan was published in 1969, again with Wilson & Wolmersley as the principal consultants. The Highways and Traffic Consultants were Jamieson & MacKay, both of whom had been traffic engineers in Hugh Wilson's team in Cumbernauld. The Israel Institute of Urban Studies under Professor Haim Ben-Shahar were also consulted on computer modelling, etc.

The finalised version of this plan for the town under the title 'The Irvine New Town Plan' was not published until 1971.

A Regional Context

One of the features of the Irvine designation, and a hallmark of its time, was its place within a much wider sub-regional 'planning for growth' context. A sub-regional plan had been prepared by the Ayrshire Land Needs Working Party under the chairmanship of Dr Dickson Mabon, the Minister of State in the Scottish Office. This saw a future population of 200,000 people being accommodated between Irvine and Kilmarnock to the east.

The New Town Starts to be Built

In the meantime it had been necessary to find land upon which housing development could get under way. This was done in the north of the designated area at Pennyburn to the west of Kilwinning. The project was inaugurated in December 1968 by the Secretary of State himself, William Ross.

Nevertheless, during the late 1960s there was criticism of the perceived slow development of Irvine. In retrospect it can be seen that the time spent at the beginning in getting things right was time well spent.

Gottries Place, Harbourside, looking east

THE PLAN

The Topography

The topography extends from a broad seaboard landscape of coastal dunes and raised beaches to the slightly raised and undulating countryside of North Ayrshire. The whole overlooks Irvine Bay in the Firth of Clyde, where the waters of the river Irvine and the Annick Water flow into the sea by the estuary of the Garnock. The Designated Area omitted the Bogside area on the east bank of the river Garnock and the Ardeer peninsula to its west - occupied by the ICI Explosive Works.

Neighbourhood shops and busway, Broomlands

The Plan

The plan, as it eventually emerged in 1971, was relatively simple in concept. It provided for a new route for the A78 as a major grade-separated regional road, which both serves the town and carries traffic through it. This road runs to the east of the existing suburbs of Irvine, and to the south of Kilwinning. To the east of this road is a north/south distributor road which serves an arc of bead-like residential communities. Between the two roads there is further residential development to the north and industry to the south. The main areas of industrial development are then largely in the south of the designated area with some smaller pockets at Kilwinning.

Cheviot Way, Bourtreehill - leafy residential

THE TOWN CENTRE

The Planning Proposals

The historic centre of Irvine was at the heart of the medieval Burgh itself, whose Charter from the King granted it the right to hold a market.

The first Wilson plan of 1967 proposed that the central area of the New Town should be on a green-field site to the east

Lawthorn Farm as a pub and restaurant

The Cross and Eglinton Street at the heart of the medieval Irvine street pattern

Multi-storey car parking in New Street was a part of the original vision for the Centre

Bridgegate Square looking eastwards to the Cross, Irvine Burgh

The Rivergate Shopping Bridge seen from the south - the new inhabited bridge replaces the 19th-century Irvine Brig

of the Burgh in the valley of the Annick Water. By 1969, however, the interim revised outline plan proposed that the central area for the whole New Town should be within Irvine Burgh adjacent to the existing town centre. When the 'Irvine New Town Plan' was published in 1971 this had been refined to a proposal for a 'single-level linear shopping deck, flanked by car parks and office accommodation, extending from the existing Irvine Cross to the Railway Station'.

This concept embraced a 'Shopping Bridge' replacing the nineteenth-century Irvine Brig, and also would have made Irvine the first Scottish New Town to fully integrate the railway station within a single enclosed town centre. Although, in the event, the new centre was not to extend that far as a 'single-level linear shopping deck', the present relationship with the railway station is excellent.

The town centre scale model which was constructed and displayed at the time the plan was published has distinct echoes of the Cumbernauld town centre model of a decade earlier. The Irvine 'deck', if completed, would have connected with the similarly ambitious proposals for the redevelopment of the Irvine Harbourside.

The Shopping Bridge is Built

The first part of this centre to be built was the Shopping Bridge over the river Irvine. It was opened in 1976 with the reconstructed Bridgegate being completed later. The loss of the Irvine Brig is still keenly felt amongst older residents.

The idea, however, of an 'inhabited bridge' was in itself a very old idea with a splendid pedigree. The Old London Bridge had been a living community spanning the Thames, complete with its own resident population as well as its commercial premises. With the passing of that London Bridge, society

Housing court, Lawthorn

developed a different intellectual perspective of river bridges - they were to be seen for themselves, as a part of the river vista, rather than as obstructions to such a view. Certainly bridges were not seen as destinations in their own right. They simply allowed people to cross the river to reach the other side. It is significant that the idea of 'inhabited bridges' has recently been revived with an exhibition in London at the Royal Academy in 1996.

Irvine's Shopping Bridge was a brave statement about the town centre of Irvine. It ensured that the boundary set by the river was breached, without the inconvenience of either a draughty walk or an empty and sterile glass tunnel. It is there and it is an important 'destination'. It is home to an active trading community and to other facilities, and even if people don't actually 'live' there, it is an 'inhabited bridge'.

The Shopping Bridge

The Shopping Bridge in its fairly severe 1970s style is perhaps not great architecture. It does possess the virtue of being a simple statement lying between the Burgh Wimpey Blocks in the west, and the spire of Trinity Church in the east. At night its illumination more clearly unites the two parts of Irvine's town centre.

Internally it has recently been refurbished with a dramatic white arched and coffered blue ceiling. It is wide and welcoming, and the full-height glazing on its northern side allows a panoramic view of the river. At its eastern end it finishes in the redeveloped Bridgegate leading to Irvine Cross, and at the west end it steps down to the ground level in a glazed atrium of generous proportion.

Pedestrian path from Muirside Court to the Pennyburn Centre

Formal housing at Girdle Toll

The refurbished Rivergate Shopping Mall

The Riverway Retail Park - town centre edge retail warehouses and McDonald's Restaurant

The Western Centre

The greater part of the car parking is located here in both surface and multi-storey form. There is an Asda store and a series of other public buildings and offices, and to the south the adjacent Riverway Retail Park - the entrance of which is marked by a McDonald's Restaurant.

All of this is a departure from the concept in the plan of 1971, but it nevertheless has allowed a contemporary and attractive centre to evolve which is entirely complementary to the Shopping Bridge. Through this area passes the wide pedestrian route to the buses and trains, before continuing beneath the refurbished railway station, to the Harbourside.

Irvine Burgh

If the treatment of the Bridgegate and the demolition of the old Brig were controversial actions by the Development Corporation, its care of the historic core of the Burgh has been widely commended for its sensitivity. There is careful infill, restoration of the best of the old, faithful renewal of the groundscape, the use of complementary urban landscape and much else. Glasgow Vennel, Hill Street and Seagate are just three examples of the Development Corporation's gentle hand

The railway station to Glasgow lies between the town centre and the Harbourside

The Glasgow Vennel, Irvine Burgh, restored by the Development Corporation and Cunninghame District Council - the poet Robert Burns once lived here

'Causies and cobbles' in the Seagate, Irvine Burgh - 'conservation and enhancement' by the Development Corporation. The Street contains the 16th-century Seagate Castle

The Glasgow Vennel restoration, Irvine Burgh

in restoring the heart of the old Irvine Burgh.

Once threatened with being a sideshow, the Burgh is now at the heart of the New Town. In this sense the New Town is Irvine; that is by right of history, as well as of designation.

Kilwinning Burgh

Irvine New Town, however, also contains the smaller Burgh of Kilwinning with its Cross and High Street, and the ruins of the medieval abbey. Another town centre! The congested High Street was pedestrianised in 1983 and has subsequently seen some sensitive development of infill sites, especially the Abbeygate Housing, completed in 1996, the architecture of which bears more than a hint of similarity to the concurrent Harbourside housing.

The historic Hill Street, Irvine Burgh - now pedestrianised

Also in Kilwinning is the YMCA/YWCA facility completed in the mid-1980s and since honoured with Design Awards by an array of groups with an interest in good design: amongst them the RIBA, the RIAS and the Saltire Society. Sadly the buildings have now found different uses as a church and amenity housing.

THE HARBOURSIDE

In 1996 the Royal Town Planning Institute gave a 'commendation' to the Development Corporation for its Harbourside development, as a part of its 'Annual Awards for Planning Achievement'. The judges commented that the fruits of the Corporation's efforts, 'over a long and sustained period were evident in the quality and popularity of the urban environment created'.

Infill housing adjacent to Glasgow Vennel, Irvine Burgh

It could, however, have been so very different.

The 'other' ancient Burgh - Kilwinning High Street - now pedestrianised. Nearby is the ruined Kilwinning Abbey from the 12th-century, and the adjacent 18th-century Parish Church with an early 19th-century detached tower

Underpass from the town centre to the harbourside runs beneath the railway station

Archway entrance to the Scottish Maritime Museum, Harbourside

The 'Linthouse' Engine Shed, Scottish Maritime Museum, Harbourside - the shed came from Stephen's of Linthouse Yard, Govan

The 'Customs House' looking towards Gottries Place - a courageous reinvention of a 'might have been' past

Portico detail on the 'Customs House'

Heritage Square and Gottries Road

The 1971 plan saw the development of the Harbour and Foreshore as both an important leisure location, and as a natural extension to the town centre. The difference, however, between the concrete mega-structures in the contemporary sketches by David Gosling, and the present wholly delightful blend of the old and the new, are testimony to the Corporation's ability to reflect the social changes of the succeeding 25 years.

The centrepiece of this resurrected Harbourside is the Heritage Square at the heart of the Scottish Maritime Museum. It is bounded by the large Linthouse engine shed transferred here from Glasgow, and by the buildings in Heritage Street. The principal building of this group is the Customs House, a simple three-storey building in early nineteenth-century style and with a central recessed classical portico. The dignity of this formal green building dominates the Square and its larger Linthouse neighbour. It is backed by a triangle of carefully proportioned and well-executed traditional housing. It is the focal point of the scene when viewed along Gottries Road.

If the construction of faithfully detailed new 'old' buildings was the primary objective of Harbourside's creators, it would appear to have been little more than an exercise in costume drama set design. Indeed, whilst the Harbourside could, quite feasibly, figure as such on our television screens, its true integrity and merit derive from its placement next to some exceptionally fine modern housing, both in terraces and flats. These cream-rendered buildings retain a simplicity which is both delicate in detail and robust in conception. Whilst remaining essentially modern, these structures possess a nautical demeanour overlaid by 1930s Art Deco. They sit happily alongside the 'heritage' housing and share with it the outstanding paving, street furniture and iron artwork.

'Customs House' Square, Harbourside - a well-cobbled treatment for a make-believe 'heritage' square

The Harbourside

Along the waterfront the dockside has been extensively upgraded, and gives access to the pontoons to the Scottish Maritime Museum's floating exhibits. There is a life-sized *Carter and his Horse* in bronze by David Annan as a reminder of all the years during which goods came ashore in medieval Irvine and were hauled by horse and cart to Glasgow. The dockside is backed by a mixture of new, refurbished and older properties including a public house known as The Oldest Pub in Irvine.

A 'traditional' terrace of new houses off 'Customs House' Square

The Oldest Pub in Irvine, Harbour Street

Gable view of New Flats in Gottries Place, Harbourside

The Carter and his Horse, a full-size bronze by David Annan, Harbourside

The Magnum Centre

Only the Magnum Leisure Centre, opened in 1976, is in the uncompromising 1960s style of architecture which was once thought appropriate for the Harbourside. A regional draw

The Magnum Centre, Harbourside, built by the old Irvine Burgh Council

Low-lying Irvine from its river

The Caledonian Paper Mill, seen from Marine Drive

Red Cross House, Irvine Burgh

for leisure activities it was built by the Burgh and designed by their architect, Ian Campbell. It is further testimony to the Town Council's ability to procure good things for the people of Irvine, and will for ever be associated with 'Mr Magnum' - Councillor Jack Carson, who fought tirelessly for it.

THE TOWNSCAPE

The townscape of Irvine is essentially that of a historic seaside Burgh and its surrounding settlements which have been renewed and extended in such a manner as to produce a greater whole, which is unique in its attractions.

There are few vantage points from which this low-lying town can be viewed in its entirety. There are snatches of views back over Irvine itself from the ring of residential settlements around the eastern periphery, and the undulating country in the east does provide contained townscapes. From the historic Dundonald Tower, however, just outside the designated area to the south the town is seen extending from the seashore to the gentle low foothills, and all set amidst trees and with a backdrop of the distant hills to the north. The mid-skyline is punctuated by the spires and tower blocks of Irvine Burgh, and there is a foreground of modern factories riding above woodland and fields.

The fabric of Irvine is essentially a blend of the historic old with the new communities running out into the pastoral landscape of the adjacent countryside. Contained within it are the many fine new buildings which have come with the New Town, such as the Red Cross House adjacent to the town centre, and a number of excellent sheltered housing and community facilities.

There is an extensive network of open space running through the designated area: fingers of green along pedestrian routes and major parks from Beach Park to Eglinton Country Park. The new housing settlements are firmly contained within structural landscape, as are the major roads and distributors.

Town Art

Like Livingston and other towns Irvine has invested heavily in the visual arts as a catalyst for enhancing the quality of the environment of the community. To this end the Development Corporation, in association with the Scottish Arts Council, had an 'Artist in Residence' Scheme in operation since 1978. There have been seven artists and sculptors during that period working with the community and creating works which are now a delight within the townscape, and a positive contribution towards the quality of life within the town. There are too many works to list, but the following serve to illustrate:

Terrace of new housing, Gottries Place, Harbourside - delicate detail

King and Queen by Roy Fitzsimmons at Hawthorn Court, Kilwinning; *All at Sea* by Mary Bourne overlooking the sea at the Harbourside; *Ring* by David Annand at Almswell Park; and *Celtic Dragon* by Anthony Vogt & Roy Fitzsimmons in Beach Park.

HOUSING

The housing within the town centre and Harbourside has already been referred to. This is a part of a considerable outflow of innovative and attractive housing during the last decade of the Corporation's life. This is largely the work of its own architects - the continuity visible in the hallmark details of plain white render, exposed rafter ends and flamboyant wrought-iron gable infills, to be seen in different parts of the town, but particularly in the Lawthorn area.

Sheltered housing, Bryce Knox Court, Lawthorn

It represents a major departure in both architecture and layout from the 1970s housing areas represented in Bourtreehill, etc. This housing was drawn largely from the common vocabulary of the Scottish New Towns / SSHA Group. In all cases, however, the Irvine designers produced sensitive groups of houses set amidst what is now lush landscaping and characterised by a judicious use of bold colour punctuation. The design teams have always excelled at good hard landscape and edge details, and this is carried through in the later use of brick paviors within the cul-de-sac courtyards.

Three-storey housing at Crofthead, Bourtreehill - stepped roofs and a 'book end' in red

There is a strong sense of visual identity in the ambient architecture of much of Irvine's Corporation-built housing - the exception, perhaps, being the earlier work in Dreghorn and Pennyburn - that first scheme started off by none other than William Ross, Secretary of State. Pennyburn, with its regular

Early housing at Lainshaw, Muirside Road, Pennyburn

Refurbished flats at Glenapp Court, Pennyburn

Court of single-storey houses off Cheviot Way, Bourtreehill

The Village Centre, Bourtreehill

Irvine Industrial Estate

Standard industrial units, Whittle Place, South Newmoor

Entrance detail of the standard industrial units, Whittle Place, South Newmoor

squares and barren access roads, is a good place, but lacks the flair of some later areas. There has, however, been major refurbishment of some of the flats, although this serves only to highlight the poverty of the buildings of the Pennyburn Centre.

Also worth mention within the housing section is the Village Centre in Bourtreehill, with its flats over shops. A piece of 'somewhere else' from the south of England, parachuted in, and left to rot. Poor-quality blockwork and a high level of vandalism spoil what is a unique piece of integrated planning in assembling many different buildings from different ownerships into a tight urban solution.

INDUSTRY

Irvine was already up and running in terms of industry when the Development Corporation arrived upon the scene. This 'Town Council Estate', now the Irvine Industrial Estate, is still a lively and satisfactory place.

Notwithstanding, the Corporation has a long record of achievement in designing 'standard' factories on a speculative basis; from the sombre regimented affairs in Newmore South to the flamboyant light structures in light grey with large overhanging eaves in the same estate, to mirror glass and red lining in Brewster Place at Shewalton. In the latter location, at Chalmers Place, there is a delightful group of small factories with reflective glass, framed in a range of primary colours, contained within trees and undergirded with new landscape planting. In Whittle Place there is a later version of the product with low roof pitches and tracery-like details. These are all high-quality industrial locations showing again the power of good design and landscape.

Elsewhere in the Riverside Business Park there are more substantial factories, such as Escom, mostly designed by the Corporation.

There are, of course, larger employers: from Beechams to Volvo to the enormous Caledonian Paper Mill at the south of the designated area - and much more. Buildings for industry in Irvine are about the use of good design.

Standard unit, Brewster Place, Riverside Business Park

SUMMARY

It would be easy to say of Irvine that it has taken a lot of people and even more money, thirty years to add some 21,000 people to an existing population of 34,500. To say that, however, would be grossly unfair and miss the point about Irvine New Town. The population may not be as high as had been planned back in the heady days of the 1960s; the sub-regional context may not have developed in the ways anticipated; some of the 1971 plan's aspirations may not, in practice, have been realised - *but* it is just possible that this is the way our society should have tackled every such situation.

Escom Computers, Riverside Way, Riverside Business Park

What Irvine has done, it has generally done very well. It has become an exemplar to others in their quest for decent, civilised living environments. There is vandalism in places, not everything has been perfect, it certainly is far from complete - indeed if any such place can ever be 'complete' - but it is a shining star by the seaside.

It has, in the event, been a wise demonstration of the New Towns Acts of Parliament. All those who share a responsibility to create the fabric of our pre-Millennium Scotland should come here, look and learn.

High-tech business units, Chalmers Place, Riverside Business Park

Chapter Seven
PEOPLE, QUANGOS AND DEMOCRACY

The Conservatory at Calderglen Country Park, East Kilbride

Trees and incidental sculpture in Woodside, Glenrothes

***The Old Men of Hoy* by Denis Barns, Livingston, complete with litter and graffiti**

Housing and mature landscape, Abronhill, Cumbernauld

Carmondean Church of Scotland Parish Church, Livingston

Democracy and Quangos

It was the democracy of the 'people in Parliament' which set in place the legislation which enabled the designation and building of these five New Towns. Local democracy nevertheless played its part, but differing in extent from place to place. It was, however, the Secretary of State for Scotland in Cabinet who took the final decisions to build East Kilbride, Glenrothes, Cumbernauld, Livingston and Irvine. The towns have been developed by what are now known as quangos (*quasi* non-governmental *o*rganisations) with all their members appointed from time to time by the Secretary of State himself. Their accountability has been to him, and through him to Parliament.

The Development Corporation Boards have been 'cuckoos in the nest of local democracy' or, as some would say, 'geese that have laid golden eggs'. They have nevertheless counted amongst their members over the years large numbers of provosts and conveners, bailies and councillors. They have also worked closely with the local authorities who had a responsibility to provide a variety of essential services to the towns, especially towards their demise to ensure a smooth transition from quango to council.

People

Quangos and councils, however, have been comprised only of 'people', and people who have been united in their desire to see 'their' New Town succeed. In this desire they have shared a commonality with all of those other people for whom the towns have been built anyway - their populations. Be they pioneer residents who arrived with the builders, children grown to adults who know no other home, grandparents arriving to join their families, the upwardly mobile whose careers have brought them there, and so on.

A Pioneering Life

Life in the New Towns in their early days, especially those without a substantial existing community, could be exciting stuff indeed. Few facilities, difficult access, a certain amount of isolation and a great deal of mud, made for a special breed - 'New Town people'. They tended to be fierce in their defence of their communities, inclined to compensate for the lack of commercial facilities with enterprises of their own. Thus, drama groups, film clubs, theatre societies, and choirs abounded. Church congregations were formed before buildings came along, and grass roots political activity thrived. All of this, and much more, laid the foundations for living communities.

The famous 'split-level' houses in Seafar, Cumbernauld - an oasis of tranquillity and shelter

Designer People

There is one group of people, however, who are sometimes remembered only by default, as in 'Who on earth did this?' - or perhaps occasionally to wonder whose skills went to create some particular aspect of a town. Many of these people now are elderly, some even dead, others have gone on to other tasks and careers.

Simply they were the rank-and-file professionals - architects, planners, engineers, landscape architects, surveyors, technicians and artists - who designed the towns.

The upper-level 'grand' entrance to the Olympia Centre from the east, East Kilbride

There is here a future academic study to more fully understand just who they were, where they came from, what motives informed them, and so on. This short book is not that study, but there follows at least a sketch of some of those who were involved. It just cannot be everyone. It doesn't even follow that the author considers those mentioned more important than others - these are simply a representative sample of the 'designer people' - particularly architects. Also, it does not attempt to include the many private consultants who have played their part. Practices, however, such as Philip Cocker & Partners; Gillespie, Kidd & Coia; and Wheeler & Sproson must never be forgotten for the part they played in the early days of the towns.

Children's play area north of Newcastle Primary School, Glenrothes

A Post-War Generation

In the early days of the towns they were exclusively men at senior levels, because the revolution which was to overtake the design professions in terms of the entry of women, was only then just beginning. In the early days, certainly in East Kilbride, Glenrothes and Cumbernauld, they were largely men who had spent at least five years of their lives 'at War'. Often they had come home to resume their professional studies, sitting alongside youngsters out of school, having put aside their wartime 'rank'.

Local shops, Lawthorn, Irvine

They were a key part of that 'generation of hope' who came back to civilian life believing that a better society than that which then existed could be created. If politicians were, as we have seen, dreaming dreams and giving effect to visions, then these designers were the willing foot soldiers of the new future.

A popular venue: the McDonald's Restaurant, Queensway, East Kilbride

The Brand Rex Factory, Viewfield Industrial Estate, Glenrothes

The Ferns public house, Ladywell, Livingston - with Spanish arches

Restaurant, pub and 'copper still' at the Nerston Roundabout, East Kilbride

Their faith in that future was to influence the generations which succeeded them for at least five decades.

Most of them lived within the towns which they were helping to create. They and their families shared the same discomforts that were experienced by all. Their children attended the same schools. Their commitment was to the same clubs, societies and churches, which formed the bedrock of these new and growing communities. Many live there still in their retirement.

One Scottish architect of this generation was to recall, 'We had a kind of feeling that we wanted to build a brave new world.' It is not the sort of sentiment which sits happily with the received wisdom of our modern world as we approach the Millennium. It does, however, encapsulate the feelings of the times for many who were there.

EAST KILBRIDE

East Kilbride's early days are remembered for the traditional nature of its design office, in which some of the younger architects felt that they played a subservient role to the town planners and engineers. Particularly at that time the layouts of housing areas was done by these two latter professions.

D.P.Reay, the first Chief Architect & Planner, left the Corporation once the master plan was resolved. He was succeeded by F.C.Scott who had previously been with Glasgow Corporation Housing Department. Eventually he also left, taking with him his depute, Lewis Fraser, and Jack Browning, one of the group leaders of the early architectural teams. The practice which they formed was Scott, Fraser & Browning, who in due course went on to design the Civic Centre for East Kilbride Burgh Council. Other architects particularly remembered for their contributions were Gus Maude, an Australian, Tom King, Andy Gundall and Innes Taggart.

The town centre from the edge: the Plaza Tower and multi-storey parking from Rothesay Street, East Kilbride

GLENROTHES

Glenrothes, by comparison, worked from the beginning within a multi-disciplinary 'studio', in which the different professions shared the same work area.

The first Chief Architect & Planning Officer was E.A.Ferriby who stayed for only a few months before leaving to take up a similar position in Bracknell New Town in England. He was succeeded by the better-remembered Peter Tinto, whose influence upon the town was considerable.

Glenrothes was noteworthy, although not unique, for the length of time which design staff tended to spend there. Many from the early days were to spend their whole careers there, and still live within the town. Thus architects such as Sandy Watson, George Leitch, John Coghill and Jack Baird were amongst many whose contributions represented a greater part of their careers.

Tinto was followed by Merlyn Williams, a Welshman, who took the town through much of its middle years. He in turn was succeeded by John Coghill, an internal promotion, and he in turn by Jack Baird. Last was Sandy Bannerman who had been in both Cumbernauld and Northern Ireland.

Coloured render in Pitteuchar, Glenrothes

Hippos are at large in Riverside Park, Glenrothes

'Articulate and confident': Glenrothes High School

CUMBERNAULD

Cumbernauld represented something of a departure. Hugh Wilson built up an enormously capable and talented team, many from outwith Scotland. It was something of a 'hot-house' atmosphere, located in the William Adam mansion, Cumbernauld House; work frequently spilled over to the village pub and to people's homes. There was a social cohesion amongst them, and many have remained friends to this day.

Mostly they did not remain in Cumbernauld for very long.

Craigmarloch Lodge public house in suburban roadhouse style, Cumbernauld

A tracery of steel on the football stadium, Broadwood, Cumbernauld

Carrickstone Vale private housing seen from the Hilltop, Cumbernauld

Pedestrian pend in 1960s terrace housing, Smithyends, Cumbernauld

The town began to receive international publicity at a time when the next round of New Towns were being designated, principally in England. Hugh Wilson's men were suddenly in demand. Wilson himself went off into private consultancy with Lewis Wolmersley from Sheffield. His hand was subsequently to be seen in the master plans for Irvine, Redditch and Northampton New Towns. He was succeeded in 1963 in Cumbernauld by one of his own team, Dudley Leaker, who himself went to Warrington in 1969, and eventually to Milton Keynes.

George Jamieson and Bill MacKay, traffic engineers, went into private consultancy and have since achieved international success as Jamieson & MacKay, Engineering Consultants. Bill Gillespie, the landscape architect who had collaborated with the consultant Peter Youngman on the landscape design of the town, left to form Gillespies, now one of the country's principal Environmental Design Consultants.

For a generation this group were to be found throughout the British urban design establishment and their influence must be regarded as considerable. Some went further afield to other countries, to the United States, to Australia and New Zealand.

At least eight went to be chiefs in their own right, or into other senior positions in other situations - mostly New Towns, and all of them outwith Scotland. Some did eventually return, amongst them Sandy Bannerman to be Chief at Glenrothes, Harry Eccles to SSHA, Roy Hunter to teach at Strathclyde University, Derek Lyddon to be Chief Planner in the Scottish Office, and Gerry Callaghan after retiring from Northampton.

Ken Davie, who had joined Wilson's team from College, became Chief in Cumbernauld in 1970, a position he held until his retirement in 1993. It was Davie who brought the

High-density housing with flat roofs in north Carbrain, Cumbernauld

'second' generation into being in Cumbernauld and who with others lent it the continuity which other towns had enjoyed; people such as Ken Johnston, son of an Edinburgh architect, and Malcolm Allen, who was previously in Glenrothes, and many others.

LIVINGSTON

Livingston brought another visionary architect and planner into the Scottish New Towns in the form of Peter Daniel. Like Reay in East Kilbride, however, he was to leave once the initial master plan process had been concluded. He was followed in 1966 by Bill Newman Brown who had come to Livingston as project architect on the Cameron Iron Works. He lent to Livingston the important mid-term stability, retiring in 1982, when he was succeeded by Gordon Davies who had been engaged on the abortive Stonehouse project for East Kilbride. Again the Livingston team enjoyed stability and continuity. Oddly, there were few if any people who moved directly from Cumbernauld to Livingston.

Bleak shopping square, Deans Village, Livingston

Single-storey houses in Howden, Livingston

IRVINE

Irvine followed the pattern of Cumbernauld and Livingston in appointing a talented visionary as their first Chief Architect & Planner in the person of David Gosling, a young man with energy who had just spent a year and a half in Brasilia.

Amongst the new team at Irvine there was further movement from Cumbernauld. The town also saw the input of both Jamieson & MacKay and Hugh Wilson himself. Irvine was at least a 'cousin' to Cumbernauld.

Plain terrace, Knightsridge, Livingston

Irvine, like others, had continuity. Two 'lists' of staff can be compared. The first in the 1971 plan, and the second in the 1996 'celebration' brochure. Six names are common to the two lists. Including Gosling there were three Chief Architects & Planners. John Billingham followed Gosling before moving to Oxford. Ian Downs, ex-Cumbernauld, who came to Irvine in 1979 from the West Midlands County Council, brought innovative continuity to the Design Team for a period of seventeen years. On his retirement in 1996 George Wren became Chief Architect.

A Life after New Towns?
By the time the East Kilbride team came to design the abortive Stonehouse, the Chief Architect & Planner was Richard Colwell, supported by, amongst others, Gordon Davies. At the demise of Stonehouse, Colwell and many of his team were transferred to the Scottish Development Agency to work on the Glasgow East Area Renewal. This provided the first

Landscape and housing, Kildrum, Cumbernauld

Three-storey terrace in Deans, Livingston

Satellite dishes, Knightsridge, Livingston

Residential Home, Bourtreehill, Irvine

'planned' movement of a New Town design team into the 'renewal' of a parent city. There was a strong sense that East Kilbride had come home.

The movement of other senior staff from New Town to Local Government appears to have been limited, until the transfer to the successor authorities of some of the remaining planning, architectural and landscape staff at the wind-up of the Corporations. Amongst the individual exceptions were Jack Hugh who was depute to Gordon Davies in Livingston, and went to be Depute City Architect in Glasgow, and Roger Pead who went from being a planner at Irvine to Depute Director of Planning in Strathclyde Region. Also during the 1980s Fife Regional Council had both a Director and Assistant Director of Architectural Services who had come out of the Scottish New Towns, respectively Cumbernauld and Glenrothes.

Recognition?

Recognition comes in many ways, but for the designers of the New Towns it has perhaps always been most important that it was their work which was recognised, rather than themselves.

The work has been recognised by many bodies for many years. The Saltire Society alone having made some forty Awards for 'Housing Design' in the Scottish New Towns, and other awards have been referred to in the foregoing sections. All of this masks the fact that, generally speaking, the New Town designers have been largely self-effacing and anonymous, feeling that the judgement of the residents of the towns was perhaps the most important criterion by which they should be judged.

Of the forty Saltire Awards, however, sixteen have been given to Irvine, including the housing in Harbour Street. It perhaps is not surprising, therefore, that at the end of 1996 two

Safeway and car parking at the Carmondean Neighbourhood Centre, Livingston

of the Irvine Team, George Wren and Roan Rutherford, were awarded the 'Best Architect' Award in the new Architectural Awards set in place by the organisers of the annual 'Scotbuild' Exhibition. Presenting the Awards, Andrew Wright, President of the Royal Incorporation of Architects in Scotland, said of Wren, 'He has set standards of excellence, achieved in an entirely practical manner, ensuring always that building programmes are designed to time-scales and budgetary constraints.' Of Rutherford he said, 'With a distinguished career and a succession of beautiful buildings, Roan Rutherford's architecture is firmly rooted in the modern tradition of space, light and natural materials, yet, like Mackintosh, draws its inspiration from Scottish traditional buildings and their methods of construction.'

George Wren is the last Chief Architect of Irvine.

Roan Rutherford, whose public architecture in Irvine has defined a generation, is the son of the late Tom Rutherford, an award-winning public-sector architect in Fife.

This event seems a fitting end to the cascade of professional talent which has been such a large part of the New Town story in Scotland.

New houses in Harbourside, Irvine - 'maritime' modern

The 'village street', Balloch, Cumbernauld

The Clydesdale Bank and Court Buildings on Almondvale Boulevard, Livingston

Postscript
CHANGE AND...?

Wrought-iron *Maid* and rental housing, Lawthorn, Irvine

'Pristine after forty years': Auchmuty High School, Glenrothes

Time to Look by Andrew Mylius, Livingston

The above words start a line within a well-known hymn by Francis Henry Lyte. The full text being, 'Change and decay in all around I see'. They are used here because often we are encouraged by some commentators to believe that a large part of what has been built in post-war Britain has been a failure, especially if it was built by the public sector.

This short book suggests that however true this might be in general terms, there are five New Towns in Scotland which epitomise the successful best that a benevolent and enabling 'caring State' has been able to achieve. That State provided patronage of architecture and enabled a whole post-war generation of designers who themselves believed in the creation of a better future for the society of which they were a part.

The visitor to these towns will make their own judgement as to their success, or indeed their failure. For a quarter of a million people, however, they are home, and because they are home, their people have a vested interest in their sustainability as good places to live.

The Climate of Change

Sustainability, however, is not about never changing. Fifty years is half a century, and anyone alive now who was a young adult at the end of the Second World War knows only too well the degree to which our society has been subjected to change. There is an inevitability about change. For urban environments, however, the issue is as much about being able to manage change as being able to survive it. The commentator Charles Jencks described the city as 'an uncanny organism, a slime mould'. Perhaps this is true to a degree of any urban community, not only is it always changing because society itself is changing, but much of that change will be unpredictable.

The origins of the five Scottish New Towns belong in time to that period when society believed that 'change' could be both predicted and managed. Perhaps that is still true, but how we go about it has changed also.

The New Towns were at their beginning prescribed by 'plans', 'master' or otherwise. This could easily mean that they would by now be 'frozen abstractions', unchanged from their first days and unable to cope. In this scenario they would be a sort of urban time-machine moving through the wreck of changing social history, to arrive into our contemporary society with as much relevance as cavalry on the Somme!

There are places like that.

It has not happened in these five New Towns.

Instances of Change

Governments have used 'their' New Towns to demonstrate changes in their own policies - principally in Scotland to use them as tools in their efforts to attract 'inward investment' and to regenerate the Scottish economy. Taken together with other broader changes within our society over fifty years this has meant that the New Towns as they are now to be experienced are very different places from the ones envisaged at their designation.

There are too many examples of change to encompass here, but three will illustrate:

Industrial Policy

At the beginning of the Scottish New Towns, Government did not envisage them building factories to attract incoming industry. In time, however, this view could not be sustained and the Development Corporation 'advance' factory, often innovative in design, became a pioneer of a wider change in Scotland: 'Come and locate your business here - we have a place ready and waiting for you to start your operation and in which to offer employment to our people.'

Community

At the beginning also the New Towns were anxious to interpret their 'balanced' communities as places of considerable social and cultural unity. Places in fact in which inhabitants of differing social station would live together, enriching each other's lives and sharing common services. In reality the New Towns were amongst the first to sell their rented houses at discounted prices to those tenants who could afford it - even before this became a wider Government policy. This began the process of separation within the New Town communities. Through the building of 'executive' housing to the present 'developer' enclaves, the New Towns are not strangers to their people's desire to have a home of some style.

Innovation

All the Scottish New Towns have seen themselves, to a greater or lesser degree, as innovators in terms of architecture and urban design. That spirit of creativity has never been extinguished, and indeed has in places burned brightly until the end. Perhaps the town centre in Cumbernauld was

The Burroughs factory at Wardpark, Cumbernauld, now refurbished for OKI

Safeway superstore occupies a retail park site vacated by industry at Queensway, Glenrothes

Business units in Riverside Business Park, Irvine - clear line horizontal

Vivid blue and green grass - factory in Kirkton Campus, Livingston

Woodside Neighbourhood Centre - the first in the town, Glenrothes

'Traditional' new houses in Harbourside, Irvine

retrospectively to be the point after which pragmatism was to be blended more acutely with that creativity. In truth, none of the town centres of these New Towns is what was originally conceived for them. They have each had to change as they developed, in order to accommodate the social, economic and retailing norms of their day.

Can the New Towns Live?

The 1971 Irvine New Town Plan observed that 'for a town to be socially successful and visually attractive it must be prosperous'. Prosperous communities are able to afford to continue to invest and reinvest in the fabric of their communities. The New Towns were always to be balanced communities in which their residents had the opportunity to be employed and financially active, as well as to live.

Their fabric was also to be of a good quality which would allow graceful ageing rather than degradation. In 1973 Oliver Cox wrote in a UK submission to the 'UN Seminar on New Towns' that 'Architecture is not what New Towns are primarily about, though as an observer can readily testify, the towns have a lot of it to show.'

The Scottish New Towns have thus aspired to high ideals. Good 'urban design' dignifies the corporate life of the inhabitants of a place, contributing towards a social identity and culture and the importance of 'place' within the human experience. At best this leads to an 'ownership' which is beyond legal ownership, but an ownership which says, 'I belong', and from there all can say, 'We belong' or 'This place belongs to us'.

This may be defined in terms of 'townscape'. Good townscape provides opportunity for an external and communal life for the people of a particular place and embraces an appreciation of art, sculpture and architecture. It also provides shelter, stimulating interest in the physical scene, providing space for recreation and trade, commerce and movement. It

Factories and pedestrian way in Westfield, Cumbernauld

'Authoritarian modern': the new Fife Constabulary HQ on the former Burrough's Machines site in Detroit Road, Glenrothes

Mature terrace in Deans, Livingston

enhances our visual stimulation and offers a visible expression of our culture and civilisation.

The creation also of new 'landscapes' within the town build upon and enhance the wider landscape of the area and help us in the formation of spaces and places which are friendly to our species. They act as lungs into which people can expand on warm and sunny days. They provide shelter from the rains and winds of winter. They allow us a contact with the seasons of a natural world from which our civilisation so quickly separates us. We all of us enjoy urban scenes which allow a touch of nature to invade the street: trees and flowering shrubs, grass and flowers, light and shade, and each in their rhythm and time. In this way our lives are enhanced, a part of our souls fed.

The Scottish New Towns have aspired to these ideals and amidst all the many constraints laid upon them have sought to bring them to fruition.

Single-storey housing in Pennyburn, Irvine

The Future

If there is a proper concern in the lives of these New Towns, it has to be the fear that the mosaic of new ownership patterns, deprived of the unifying authority of their single-minded Development Corporations, will be unable to underpin their communities with the care to which they have become accustomed.

Sustaining urban environments is, anyway, at the end of the day about 'caring' for what we have. It does not happen despite ourselves. It is an act of 'will' on the part of our society: the will to achieve the standards set out here; the will to sustain economically viable communities; the will to invest resources in the public estate as well as the private; the will to continue to embrace change; the will to share a place which is common to us all; the will to care about the communities within which we live.

There are no built environments which somehow take care of themselves - we have to care for them.

Refurbished flats in Ladywell, seen from the pedestrian bridge over Cousland Road, Livingston

Could there be Another Future?

If many people in Scotland are unaware as to which towns are meant when we speak of the 'New Towns', then it is because there has been an explosion of urban development within our countryside in recent years. This has happened, and is happening, without the advantages enjoyed by the New Town Development Corporations; in particular, their power to purchase land at 'existing use value', and to thus devote the 'accrued value' to the benefit of the wider community.

The New Towns Acts are still available, should Government see the desirability of their use. The problems have not gone away...

Standard unit, Riverside Business Park, Irvine

The refurbished Harbourside, Irvine - a reminder of past glories

Appendix A
THE 'PARKER MORRIS STANDARDS'

Houses in Bourtreehill, Irvine, look out to a green landscaped 'lung'

Simple semis in The Murray, East Kilbride

House at Weavers Brae, Craigmarloch, Cumbernauld

For a generation Sir Parker Morris LL.B was to have his name indelibly associated with generous space standards in British housing. These were the 'Parker Morris Standards'.

Sir Parker Morris was the Chairman of a Public Committee set up by Government in 1958, 'to consider the standards of design and equipment applicable to family dwellings and other forms of accommodation, whether provided by public authorities or by private enterprise, and to make recommendations'.

The sponsor was the Minister of Housing and Local Government in London, but in course of time the Committee's recommendations, published in 1961, were to find their way into the 'Housing Space Standards' documents and 'Statutory Building Regulations' over the whole UK.

Although appointed by an English Minister, the members of the Committee made one trip to Scotland to visit Cumbernauld, which was just beginning to demonstrate its early and radical approach to housing design - although, curiously, Cumbernauld Development Corporation made no submission to the Committee, either written or oral.

In their Report the Committee stated that 'an increasing proportion of people are coming to expect their home to do more than fulfil the basic requirements. It must be something of which they can be proud; and in which they must be able to express the fullness of their lives.' It was a generous statement which was to find itself in sympathy with the generation of the 'swinging sixties', and especially with the Labour Government which assumed office in 1964, not to mention the architects of the Scottish New Towns. The origins of the Report, however,

Private semis, Dedridge, Livingston

lay within the Macmillan years of the 1950s - 'You have never had it so good.'

In particular, the Committee identified two major changes which needed to be made in Housing Standards in Britain - space and heating; generally it was held that there wasn't sufficient of either.

Their conclusions covered anything from the warm house to the reasonably spacious one in which contemporary living standards and patterns could be accommodated, 'the right approach to the design of a room is, first to define what activities are likely to take place within it'!

They advocated everything from adequate storage space to good landscape design, and were open in their advocacy of the architectural profession:

> There are many standard plans of houses and flats, but to imply one or other of them in ordering the building is to lose half of the advantage of employing an architect; for not only does it do half his work for him - it also restricts his scope, and makes new and worthwhile developments in house design all the less likely.

Notwithstanding, in Scotland a sort of standardisation in house design was reached in the 1970s with the work of both the Scottish Special Housing Association (SSHA) and the Scottish Local Authorities Special Housing Unit (SLASH). Both these groups were closely associated with the New Towns Housing Architects Group. The collective influence can be seen in housing design in all of the Scottish New Towns during this period.

In 1981 the Parker Morris Standards were scrapped by Michael Heseltine, then the new Secretary of State for the Environment, the view being taken that the 'market' would decide in future on housing standards.

In the subsequent years there has been a seed change in housing in Britain with the virtual death of Local Authority or Development Corporation building of general needs housing, and the rise of the Housing Associations and Private Sector.

The house-building industry, however, in the form of the National Housing Federation, has sponsored a study by the Joseph Rowntree Foundation which was published in early 1997 under the title *The Guide to Standards and Quality*. This deals with the issue of 'space standards for housing' and aims to 'raise the minimum space standards of housing association properties'.

We have come full circle! If Scotland is to address its need for social housing in the future, then it will need to have adequate housing standards.

Sitting in the sun - Lawthorn, Irvine

Tall housing climbing the hill in Dedridge, Livingston

Tonal roughcast render at Copenhagen Avenue, East Kilbride

Appendix B
HOUSING STANDARDS

Semi-detached bungalows, Lawthorn, Irvine

Housing, trees and shelter, Geddes Hill, East Kilbride

Housing in a mature landscape in Woodside, Glenrothes

The 'Y' plan flats in Kildrum, Cumbernauld - the 'Y' refers to the plan configuration

For most of the post-war period in which rented housing has been built in Scotland by Local Authorities and New Town Development Corporations, the Government of the day has sought to protect and maximise the investment made by the public purse through the establishing of 'Standards' which have had to be adhered to by all those seeking to 'borrow' money from the Public Loan Board (the Exchequer).

Thus, during the period when substantial numbers of houses were being built, the controlling documentation in Scotland, and published by the Scottish Office, has been the *Scottish Housing Handbook*. This has covered such subjects as: housing layout, roads & services, house design, the equipment of houses, tenders & specifications, multi-storey housing, and housing procedure.

The revised edition of 1958 (*Housing Layout*) defined the 'Purpose of the Handbook as a whole' thus: 'it brings together in a convenient form the standards of layout, roads, house design and equipment required for housing schemes of local authorities. It also indicates how a high quality of design and appearance may be achieved with economy. At the same time it leaves the authorities scope for designing their schemes so as to satisfy local needs and tastes.'

Such was the background against which the New Towns began their task.

The specific function of the *Handbook* was described as being 'to set out the Department's requirements and recommendations for...housing schemes'.

Big brother was indeed watching!

With the coming of metrication on 1 January 1969, the opportunity was taken to prepare the *New Scottish Housing Handbook*.

A new document on 'Metric Space Standards' was issued in 1968 in anticipation of the coming change, and was itself a replacement for Part 3 of the *Scottish Housing Handbook: House Design*, which had been published in 1956.

The old standards were seen to 'have generally proved adequate', but 'changing social needs, and the mass of new information on all aspects of Housing Design and Layout, which has emerged from research studies', were cited as evidence of the need to produce new and improved standards.

To coincide with the introduction of the new 'metric space standards', a new 'system of cost planning and indicative costs for local authority housing' was introduced to be effective from 1 January 1969. It was said that 'the basic principle of the system is that by means of published tables of indicative costs, local authorities will know, from the outset of planning their housing proposals, the level of cost which will be accepted for the purpose of subsidy'.

For the Development Corporations, committed to innovative design and high quality, it was a continuation of the stranglehold which had been present in Government financing of housing since the beginning. It just became even more difficult, and what had been known as 'cost yardsticks' took on the rather more sinister title of 'indicative costs'.

Since all the monies, anyway, came from the Exchequer the subsidy level was vital.

Whilst the 'space standards' themselves were generous - at least in terms of later developments - the 'indicative costs' were draconian, and could really only be achieved at the expense of building quality and thus sustainability.

Terraced houses in Howden, Livingston - seen from the Bridges Path

> The published tables show the costs for which dwellings of given sizes and built to given densities can reasonably be provided. The costs do not relate to a dwelling of a given shape, construction or specification; they represent instead the upper limit of expenditure which is reasonable to incur to meet a given housing requirement, having regard to the standards to which housing is built, the density of development and the average size of the families accommodated.

This injunction was followed by the honeyed words, that 'within this upper limit of expenditure the designer has a considerable degree of freedom to decide ...'.

Well, that depends!

Although it was possible within limits to negotiate special allowances for such things as unusual foundations or underbuildings, the 'indicative cost' paid scant attention, for instance, to the need for high standards of hard and soft landscape design - the provision of which became a hallmark of housing in the Scottish New Towns.

Officials within the Scottish Office were apt to make reference to the much lower 'landscape' costs being achieved by the Local Authorities in their Housing Developments.

Sometimes people ask why building quality did not always follow innovative design. The foregoing will go some way to explain.

Mature trees in Bourtreehill, Irvine

Housing in north Carbrain, Cumbernauld

Bibliography

BOOKS
ADAMS, Ian H, *The Making of Urban Scotland*, 1978
BRIGGS, Asa, *Victorian Cities*, 1968
BROADY, Maurice, *Planning for People*, 1968
BROGDEN, W A, *The Neo-Classical Town*, 1996
CAMERON, James T, *East Kilbride - Scotland's First New Town*, 1996
CARTER, Christopher, *Innovations in Planning Thought and Practice at Cumbernauld New Town 1956-62*, 1983
CARTER, Christopher & KEATING, Michael, *The Designation of Cumbernauld New Town*, 1986
CHATIN, Catherine, *9 Villes Nouvelles*, 1975
CHERRY, Gordon E, *The Evolution of British Town Planning*, 1974
CLOSE, Rob, *Ayrshire & Arran - An Illustrated Architectural Guide*, 1992
DOWNS, Ian, *Irvine New Town 1966-96*, 1996
FERGUSON, Keith, *A History of Glenrothes*, 1982
FITZSIMMONS, Jack, *Bungalow Bliss*, 1993
GEDDES, Sir Patrick, *Cities in Evolution*, 1968
GORDON, George & DICKS, Brian, *Scottish Urban History*, 1983
HEAP, Desmond, *The New Towns Act 1946 - Annotated*, 1947
HOLLEY, Stephen, *Washington - Quicker by Quango*, 1983
HORSEY, Miles, *Tenements & Towers*, 1990
HOWARD, Ebenezer, *Garden Cities of Tomorrow*, 1902
JAQUES, Richard & McKEAN, Charles, *West Lothian - An Illustrated Architectural Guide*, 1994
KEATING, Michael and MIDWINTER, Arthur, *The Government of Scotland*, 1983
KELLY, John, *What's A Hippo Doing in Fife?* (year not listed)
LIVINGSTON DEVELOPMENT CORPORATION, *A Place of Our Own - The Scottish New Towns*, 1991
LYDDON, Derek, *New Towns Record - Cumbernauld*, 1995
McHARG, Ian L, *Design With Nature*, 1969
MERLIN, Pierre, *New Towns - Regional Planning Developments*, 1971
MUMFORD, Lewis, *The City in History*, 1961
NASMITH, Robert J, *The Story of Scotland's Towns*, 1989
PATERSON, A B, *A Portrait of Fife* (year not listed)
PHILIPSON, Garry, *Aycliffe & Peterlee New Towns 1946-88*, 1988
PRIDE, Glen L, *The Kingdom of Fife - An Illustrated Architectural Guide*, 1990
PRIZEMAN, John, *Your House - The Outside View*, 1975
SYKES, A J M, *Cumbernauld 67 - A Housing Survey*, 1967
WILLS, Elspeth M, *Livingston - The Making of a Scottish New Town*, 1996
WOOD, Alistair J, *40 Years New Glenrothes 1948-88*, 1989

MAGAZINES & NEWSPAPERS
'On the Dock of the Bay', *Planning Week*, 30 January 1997
BUIST, Jack, 'New Hope Grows in the New Towns', *Planning Week*, 24 October 1996
'Space - The Final Front Room', *RIBA Journal*, March 1997
DAVIES, Gordon, 'Quality Built in', *Prospect*, Autumn 1996
FRANCE, Miranda, 'It's a Mall World', *Scotsman*, 24 August 1996
JENCKS, Charles, 'The City That Never Sleeps', *New Statesman*, 28 June 1996
JOHNSON, Jim and Ktystyna, 'Cumbernauld Revisited', *Architect's Journal*, 5 October 1977
LEADBEATER, Charles, 'Even Basingstoke had Style', *New Statesman*, 20 December 1996
McKEAN, Charles, 'The Way Forward for Urban Concrete - a Personal View', *Concrete Quarterly*, Autumn 1996
MEADES, Jonathan, 'From Po-Mo to So-So', *New Statesman*, 20 December 1996
New Build, 'Contractors are Open for Business', *Project Scotland*, 29 August 1996
New Build, 'Glenrothes Invests in the Future', *Project Scotland*, 27 March 1997
Scot-Build 1996, 'They're Simply the Best', *Project Scotland*, 21 November 1996
Scottish Local Authorities Special Housing Group, 'Cumbernauld - An A to Z', *SLASH Newsletter* No 6, 1976

The author has also used a considerable number of news items from the local and national press.

GOVERNMENT PUBLICATIONS
Department of the Environment, *New Towns - UN Seminar on New Towns*, 1973
Department of the Environment, *The New Towns*, 1978
Department of Health for Scotland, *Scottish Housing Handbook - Part 1 / Housing Layout*, 1958
Ministry of Housing and Local Government, *The Density of Residential Areas*, 1952
Ministry of Housing and Local Government, *Homes for Today and Tomorrow [Parker Morris]*, 1961
Scottish Development Department, *The New Scottish Housing Handbook - Bulletin 1, Metric Space Standards*, 1968
Scottish Development Department, *The New Scottish Housing Handbook - Bulletin 1 Supplementary Note - Metric Dimensional Framework*, 1970
Scottish Development Department, *Scottish Housing Handbook - Housing Development - Layout / Roads and Services*, 1977
Scottish Development Department, *Scottish Housing Handbook - Assessing Housing Need - A Manual of Guidance*, 1977

The author has also used a wide range of published and unpublished material from the Development Corporations. These include published plans, annual reports, publicity brochures, town plans and reports dealing with industry, commerce, housing, population etc.

Index